2010
Côtes de Provence

A Perennial *Feast*

Food • Flavours • Restaurants • Recipes

Text Kim Inglis
Photography Jacob Termansen

TALISMAN

Contents

A Culinary Adventure

The bespoke experience—where luxury is paired with individuality—is at the core of the culinary adventures outlined in this book. Offered at a number of YTL Hotels' properties – resorts, restaurants, hotels, food centres – around the world, they vary in cuisine and content, but are united by a common commitment to quality.

Service is key, along with a sense of place and a strong authenticity. Whether the food is Oriental or Occidental, Peranakan or Provencal, it is composed from fresh, seasonal produce and presented in a highly personalized manner. It could be a salad or sandwich in a metropolitan high-rise, a banquet on a beach, or an ice-cold cocktail on a chill-out deck: whatever the product, the surrounds are salubrious and the flavours fabulous.

YTL Hotels owns and manages a number of different hotels, resorts, restaurants and "homes away from home" that cover a wide range of locations, brands and price points. Each is very different from the next, yet they are consistent in quality, luxury, authenticity and service. The aim of this book is to share some of those experiences: focusing on the culinary offerings, explaining the different cuisines, exploring the local food philosophies and sharing some of YTL Hotel's top chefs' recipes. We hope you'll join us for the ride.

A visit to one of the hotels or resorts is always characterised by a huge variety of choice. There are the Feast Village and Fisherman's Cove restaurants that pop up in a few countries, as well as

the idiosyncratic Shook! — a restaurant that spans East and West with a powerful panache. Other offerings are site specific: Chapman's Cove on the island of Pangkor Laut is named after British Colonel Frederick Spencer Chapman who escaped from Malaya from the very beach where today's restaurant now stands and the Mansion at The Majestic Malacca, found in the dining room of this former Peranakan home, are two cases in point. They serve food suitable to site: Catch of the Day in the case of the former and some well-loved Nonya recipes in the latter.

There is variety in the cuisines too: Japanese (both in Japan and elsewhere), modern British, French, a number of regional Chinese cuisines (Cantonese, Shanghainese, Peranakan), traditional Malay, Thai and Balinese — there's even a moveable feast in the form of the delicious cuisine experienced on the famed Eastern & Oriental Express train. YTL Hotels has no reservations about offering sushi in Shanghai, Brit-style high tea in the hills of Malaysia, or Malay delicacies in a garden in Provence. Diversity is the name of the game; unusual experiences the spice of life.

One of the strengths of the various YTL Hotels' brands is the highly personalised dining experiences that are customised to individual guests. Dine in splendour beneath billowing waves of muslin on a pristine spit of sand in Borneo; have a lazy, late breakfast à deux in an open pavilion beneath the branches of century-old tropical rain forest trees; or sip champagne and sample cheeses, terrines and canapés in a garden in the South of France. If you fancy a romantic wedding anniversary dinner with a loved one or a celebration for 200, it can be arranged.

The 18th-century epicurean, Jean Anthelme Brillat-Savarin, once said that "to receive guests is to take charge of their happiness during the entire time they are under your roof". This is what YTL Hotels manages so successfully at all its venues. From the high-end Ritz-Carlton in Kuala Lumpur to the country house experience in the English village of Bray, attention to detail is paramount. Staff is on hand to attend to you when you need service; and is discreetly hidden when you want to be left alone.

The same can be said for the food: If you want a fanfare, it can be arranged; if you want something informal or casual, that's equally well catered for. Each cuisine is described in detail, and the highlights of the various restaurants are outlined. Innovative chefs have created unusual dishes and drinks: they're not shy about breaking boundaries, and are more than happy to share the tricks of their trade. It has to be said that we've left the complicated, hard-to-master recipes with the YTL Hotels' cooks in their kitchens, but have borrowed many an easier dish and presented them in the following pages. Ideal for at-home cooks, each recipe feeds six people and is simple to recreate at home. There are starters, soups, a selection of main courses, and desserts — from all corners of the globe — and a variety of drinks that harness ingredients, tastes and textures from many different sources.

The choice is yours: Create a YTL Hotels' dinner or lunch in your own home; travel to one of its exotic hotels or restaurants and experience the real thing; or do both. Whatever you decide, you can't go wrong really.

ribeye

Seafood Extravaganza

Pairing Conservation with Luxury

Covering just less than 5,000 hectares both below and above water, Sabah's Tunku Abdul Rahman Marine Park comprises five islands, vast tracts of shallow waters, colourful coral reefs, a plentiful and varied marine life, and acres of untouched tropical rain forest. As such it is the perfect place for a bit of rest and relaxation, especially if seafood is high on your list of priorities.

Of course, there is no fishing in the park itself, but there are plenty of fresh fish to be caught around Kota Kinabalu, the town that acts as the gateway to the park. In fact, the South China Sea and the waters around Sabah house some of the best sport fishing grounds in the world. You'll find an impressive variety of fish including barracuda, grouper, mackerel, marlin, and many more.

A 15-minute boat ride from the marina also takes you to Pulau Gaya and the Gaya Island Resort, an idyllic haven that pairs activity (snorkelling, nature trekking, diving, and more) with rest and relaxation. A backdrop of age-old primary rain forest frames elegant pavilion-style architecture fronting a sandy beach, fish-rich waters and views

to Mount Kinabalu, southeast Asia's highest mountain. Managing Director of YTL Corporation, Tan Sri (Dr) Francis Yeoh is keen to point out that the resort is preserving more than 65 percent of its 52-acre area intact and that construction methods were sensitively eco-friendly, even though the end result is extremely luxurious.

PREVIOUS PAGE A casual picnic is laid out on the beach; in the background the resort yacht, the Lumba-Lumba, is moored offshore.

OPPOSITE, TOP AND BOTTOM Two resort chefs prepare ingredients for the daily cooking class, where lobster is the dish of the day.

ABOVE, CLOCKWISE FROM TOP LEFT An airy pavilion overlooks the resort pool; Gaya Island Resort pier and the tranquil waters of the marine park as viewed from a villa deck; a villa block nestling amongst the rain forest; an ice cold welcome drink; a teamtime brownie is covered in white chocolate embellished with the resort's logo — very chic; a selection of cakes served in the library for tea.

Not content to rest on its laurels, the resort has embraced a line-fishing initiative in conjunction with the World Wildlife Fund, sourcing much of its seafood from fishermen that have eschewed traditional net fishing (that often traps turtles and other endangered species) for more sustainable line fishing (see photo on page 20). Gaya Island Resort's resident marine biologist is always on hand to advise — and chefs are particularly proud of the fact that they're able to cook up a feast knowing that they are supporting the local marine environment.

Naturally, as with all YTL Hotels' properties, there are a host of culinary options to consider. Two of the brand's signatures — Feast Village and Fisherman's Cove — take centre stage, but there are also poolside dining options, beach barbecues, and personalised private beach and villa experiences. Feast Village is an airy, open-

plan affair with undulating service counters, on-trend pendant lights, and a cool red-and-white palette, all enclosed within a slatted wood perimeter. Open all day, it offers a huge array of cuisines from Asia and beyond. Crab burgers, delicious salads and a variety of pasta dishes are as likely to be seen on the menu as prawns in a spicy sambal sauce and salty fried rice. Situated directly above, Fisherman's Cove specialises in seafood and shares two local Sabah recipes with us (see overleaf).

No resort worth its salt these days is without its own luxury yacht, and Gaya Island Resort doesn't disappoint with the sleek 64-footer Lumba-Lumba. Sunset cruises with canapés and main courses grilled à la minute on the upper deck are accompanied by the finest of wines and champagnes (of course). Another seafaring adventure can be had with a picnic at private Tavajun Bay; a short five-minute boat ride brings you to this private arc of white sand, where lunch is served from a traditional hamper with uniquely crafted utensils on a local coir mat. What could be more elegant yet more down-to-earth, we ask ourselves?

ABOVE, LEFT TO RIGHT The Pool Bar & Lounge is bordered by a row of undulating pillars which look out to the swimming pool and sea beyond; a walkway at dusk; a table setting at chic Feast Village makes for a pretty picture with scarlet napkins and glasses.

BELOW The elevated library is lit up at night; it has spectacular views over the marine park and to Mount Kinabalu in the distance.

OPPOSITE Fisherman's Cove features a wooden deck, private pavilion and covered dining — in a breezy elevated outdoor setting.

Pan-seared Borneo Coral Trout with Fennel & Olive Nage

Provencal in inspiration, Sabah in style. This unique, fresh-from-the-sea fish dish will tempt any palette. Remember ... when making a foamy sauce, it is best to whisk it up at the last minute (literally); and be sure to use a hand whisk, not an electronic one.

Serves 6

For the Fish

1 kg coral trout (cut into 170 g fillets per portion)
12 g Maldon sea salt
30 ml virgin olive oil
30 g unsalted butter
salt and pepper to taste

For the Vegetables

12 asparagus spears (2 per portion)
6 baby carrots (1 per portion)
6 Brussel sprouts, baby *kai lan* or any green-leafed vegetables

For the Sea Foam

800 ml good fish stock
salt to taste

For the Nage

150 g white onion, finely chopped
60 g garlic cloves, finely chopped
2 tsp fennel seeds
200 g / 1 head fennel, finely chopped
150 g black olives, deseeded and finely chopped
45 g capers, lightly smashed
5 ripe tomatoes, seeds removed and pulped to a concasse
80 ml Pernod
60 ml virgin olive oil
800 ml fish stock
30 ml lemon juice
3 tsp dill, freshly shredded
salt to taste

Method

For the fish: Heat a heavy pan over a medium-high heat. Season the fish on the meat side with salt and pepper, then, when the pan is good and hot, add the olive oil, followed by the butter. As soon as the foaming subsides, place the fish in the pan with the skin side down. Jiggle pan for the first 10 seconds to keep the fish from sticking, then cook until a golden crust forms on the skin. Carefully turn the fillets and bake in the oven at a heat of 180° C for 4 minutes.

For the nage: Sweat the onions, fennel seed and garlic in olive oil for two minutes over a low heat, then add fennel, black olives, capers, tomatoes and cook for a further minute. Add the Pernod and reduce. Add the fish stock, dill and lemon juice, then return to a simmer and season to taste.

For the vegetables: Bring a large pot of water to boil over a high heat, then just before blanching the vegetables, add a couple of tablespoons of salt to the boiling water. Salt helps to maintain colour and improve flavour, but it may be omitted if you wish. Add the vegetables to the pot, blanch each vegetable separately. Every 30 seconds, test to see if they are done. Most vegetables take between 2 to 5 minutes. When the vegetables are cooked, remove from the boiling water with a slotted spoon. Set aside.

For the foam: Heat up a small saucepan, add all the ingredients and bring to a simmer. Then, using a hand blender, whisk into a foam.

To assemble: Pour the nage into a soup plate, arrange the asparagus and carrot in the centre. Place the fish on top and spoon the sea foam on and around. Serve immediately.

Snapper Hinava

Similar to Peruvian ceviche, this excellent, tart starter has been prepared and consumed in Sabah since time immemorial. The teeming waters around Borneo have given locals a variety of fish to choose from, while limes and coriander have provided the marinade. Delicious as a light starter, at-home hinava will remind you of your sojourn in Sabah.

Serves 6

For the Fish

- 360 g snapper fillets, sliced into 2.5 cm x 8 cm pieces
- 400 ml lime juice
- 60 ml ginger juice
- 120 g shallots, finely chopped
- 3 red bird's eye chillies, finely chopped
- salt to taste

For the Coriander Oil

- 50 g coriander leaves
- 25 g flat-leaf parsley leaves
- 75 ml virgin olive oil
- 75 ml corn oil
- salt to taste

For the Lemon Foam

- 240 g lemon juice
- 240 g lime juice
- 50 g castor sugar
- 10 g salt

For Garnish

- 6 limes, char-grilled
- 2 bird's eye chillies, finely sliced
- 2 shallots, finely sliced
- handful sakura mix or other herbs or any colourful cress

Method

For the coriander oil: Bring a large saucepan of salted water to the boil, then place the coriander and parsley leaves in a seive and plunge into the boiling water for 15 seconds. Remove and plunge immediately into a bowl of water filled with ice cubes. Drain the herbs, wrap in a clean tea towel and gently squeeze dry. Roughly chop and place in a blender with the olive oil. Whiz the leaves to break them down, and then add the vegetable oil and whiz for 1 minute at high speed. Leave for several hours to drain naturally through a dampened muslin or a filter-lined coffee sieve. Discard the purée and refrigerate the oil for up to 2 days, or freeze in ice cube trays for up to 3 weeks.

For the fish: Mix all the ingredients together except for the fish slices in a bowl until the salt has dissolved. Pour over the snapper and marinate for an hour.

For the lemon foam: Mix all the ingredients together and whisk until the sugar and salt dissolve. It is best to use a hand blender to achieve a foamy consistency.

To assemble: Arrange the snapper fillets and garnish on a plate, then drizzle the coriander oil and lemon foam around and on top. Serve immediately.

Fragrant Aromas, Vibrant Colours

Malay Cuisine

As Malaysia is a multi-ethnic society, with varying cultures and peoples living in one country, it isn't surprising that Malay cuisine is multi-faceted. Each region sports a regional dish — and many borrow culinary techniques and ingredients from outsiders who have either settled in the country or were involved in the spice trade of yore. As such, Malaysia has a rich gastronomic history, with Malay traditions fusing with skills introduced by Arabs, Persians, Chinese, Indians and Europeans.

Malay adaptations of curry dishes are called *kari* or *gulai*, there's *satay* (originally from Java and Sumatra), *mee* or noodle dishes with a Chinese influence. No discussion of Malay food is complete without mention of the various *kuih* (the plural is *kuih-muih*), a selection of cakes, pastries and sweets eaten as snacks, and the variety of rice dishes — *nasi lemak*, rice steamed with coconut milk, and *nasi goreng*, fried rice, being the most ubiquitous.

ABOVE Crispy banana fritters with vanilla cream from the kitchens of Tanjong Jara Resort (see overleaf).

RIGHT The line-fishing initiative started by the World Wildlife Fund and supported by Gaya Island Resort (pages 14–16) supports fishermen such as this one, who have eschewed trawling with nets for fishing by hand.

OPPOSITE The covered market at Dungun on Malaysia's east coast reveals its fresh produce. Clockwise from top right: fresh *ikan selar kuning* or yellowtail scad; mini round eggplants; crabs; *kacang botol* or winged beans; tasty local satay, skewers of grilled meat.

Even though a journey through the country reveals many signature dishes, each having their own distinctive tastes, where they are united is in their generous use of spices, most specifically lemongrass, ginger, garlic, shallots, kaffir limes and fresh chillies. Both fresh and dried spices and numerous roots are readily available, so they also feature in many dishes. *Sambal*, a condiment made from shrimp paste or *belacan*, chillies, onions and garlic, is to be found in every household, as is a spice paste called *rempah*. Sautéed in oil to bring out its flavourful aroma, the latter has a toasty spiciness that brings richness to many recipes.

Another unifying factor is the freshness of produce. As with most southeast Asian countries, the tropical heat has resulted in a cuisine that is cooked from fresh — fish freshly caught from the seas, fruit and vegetables recently plucked from the fields and woods, meat freshly culled and prepared in the *halal* way. Other important ingredients are coconut milk (*santan*) used to give dishes a rich, creamy character and tamarind paste, pulp extracted from tamarind pods, to add a sour or tangy taste most specifically to fish and seafood recipes.

As with many other Asian cuisines, nearly every Malay meal is served with rice. Unlike Western or Japanese meals, where course follows course, in a Malay meal all dishes are served at once.

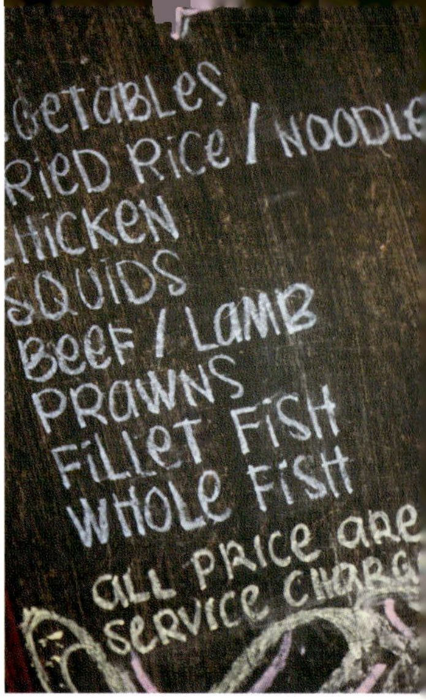

BELOW A chef demonstrates the art of de-boning and filleting a fish in a cooking class.

OPPOSITE Breakfast, with fresh juices and fruit, is laid out at one of the resort's open-air restaurants.

Unmistakably Malay

Tanjong Jara Resort

A great place to totally immerse oneself in the Malay experience — both culinary and otherwise — is Tanjong Jara Resort, a relaxed vacation spot that is steeped in age-old Malay traditions. Situated in Malaysia's heartland in Terengganu province, it is set along a coastline of fishing villages, coconut groves, white powdery sand and a sea teeming with coral and marine life.

Laidback yet luxurious, Tanjong Jara was the first deluxe tourist accommodation to be built on Malaysia's eastern coast. Its primary aims were to sustain and preserve the local architectural heritage, encourage local crafts and establish a mutually supportive relationship with nearby communities. This it has succeeded in admirably: accommodations are modelled after *istanas*, wooden palaces of great beauty and dignity built by the earlier Sultans of east coast Malaysia, the resort employs many local people, and it has immersed itself in the community with all expeditions, experiences and outings an exploration of local culture.

Di Atas Sungei

ABOVE With illumination from hurricane lamps, candles and an indigo sky, guests are invited for a private dinner on the shores of the South China Sea. The sounds of the *gamelan* and the lapping of waves enhance the romantic mood.

OPPOSITE More fresh produce from the market.

On the cuisine front, guests are encouraged to visit the local market at nearby Dungun: here they can sample local delicacies such as *keropok lekor*, a type of soft fish cracker eaten straight out of the wok and dipped in chilli sauce. Or they can bargain for local fruits, veggies and seafood, then cook them at the resort's well-established Cooking School where they'll be introduced to the creative culinary heritage of Malaysia's Malay, Chinese and Indian residents. It's a hugely instructive way to spend the day and culminates in a (hopefully) delicious meal.

All dining options celebrate the tastes and aromas of local fare. A harmonious balance of nutrition and flavour with a home-cooked touch, dishes are freshly cooked often to order. The restaurant Di Atas Sungei (Malay for "Above the River") doesn't even have a menu: Situated above the river that meanders through the resort, guests are guided by the resort's chefs who give their recommendations for the day. Another venue is Nelayan translating as "Fisherman": here, the freshest seafood is cooked in a variety of mouthwatering ways.

The Malay concept of sucimurni, which embraces tranquility and purity through wholesome living, permeates through Tanjong Jara in the same way that the river meanders through the resort — softly, slowly, quietly, with the minimum of fuss.

We share some of Tanjong Jara's culinary secrets with you overleaf — recipes for the famous Beef Rendang, a beef stew flavoured with local spices and coconut cream, and a fish dish that is sour, spicy and extremely satisfying. And since no meal is complete without a local dessert, there's a couple of sweet options as well: some of the famous *kuih-muih* and a mango soufflé: the latter may not be Malay in origin but the super local fruits couldn't get more tropical if they tried.

Beef Rendang

This rich and tender coconut beef dish is incredibly flavourful — a true Malay classic. Often served on ceremonial occasions, it cooks for a long time, so all the spices and coconut milk are fully absorbed into the meat.

Serves 6

250 ml coconut milk from 2 old coconuts
1 turmeric leaf, torn and knotted
5 Kaffir lime leaves
1 stalk lemongrass, bruised
1–2 pieces *asam gelugor* fruits (if unavailable, use juice from 2 limes)
120 g red chillies, finely sliced
1 kg beef, fat and sinew removed, cut into 3 cm cubes

selection of ground spices

45 g galangal, chopped
12 g fresh turmeric, chopped
12 g ginger, chopped
200 g red chillies, chopped
4 shallots, diced
pinch salt

Method

Mix and pound all the spices together until they are thoroughly combined.

Simmer the coconut milk with the turmeric leaf, Kaffir lime leaves, lemongrass, *asam gelugur* or lime juice, sliced chillies and ground spices until the milk thickens and becomes oily (approximately 3 minutes).

Reduce the heat, add the beef and cook for about 10 minutes until tender.

Stir occasionally until the spices dry and turn brown.

Optional: Combine *rendang* with 300 grams small potatoes. Soak potatoes in water for 15 minutes then scrub with a soft brush to clean the skins. Boil until fully cooked. Add to the gravy together with beef.

Serve with steamed rice.

Ikan Assam Pedas

Assam pedas literally translates as sour spicy, and ikan is fish — so here we've got a traditional Malay spicy fish dish that relies on the flavour of tamarind juice absorbed into the fish flesh. Every family has their own take on ikan assam pedas: Tanjong Jara's version is pungent and powerful with a sauce that is fiery hot and satisfyingly sour.

Serves 6

1 kg red snapper, cut into cubes
140 g *kesum* leaves (knotweed)
250 ml cooking oil
80 g tamarind pulp
100 g shallots
50 g garlic
50 g galangal
25 g turmeric, fresh
240 g tomatoes, cut into wedges
100 g chilli paste (from an Asian supermarket)
5 stalks lemongrass, crushed
500 ml water
5 Kaffir lime leaves
2 stalks ginger blossom, quartered

Method

Heat the oil in a large pan or wok and sauté the blended garlic, galangal, shallot and turmeric. Once well combined, add the chilli paste, lemongrass, Kaffir lime leaves — and sauté for a further 2 minutes.

Pour in the tamarind pulp and water, bring to the boil.

Place the pre-cut fish and quartered ginger blossom in the wok, season with salt, and simmer for 15 minutes. Add the tomatoes and *kesum* leaves, simmer for a minute and remove from the heat. (NB: Vegetables like eggplant, lady's fingers and/or cabbage can be added if liked.)

Serve immediately with steamed rice.

Kuih Ketayap

The beautiful green colour of this doughy snack comes from the pandan leaf addition, while the taste is sweetly coconut flavoured. It's ideal as a snack, hot or cold, at any time of the day.

Makes 15 pieces

For the Batter
180 g plain flour
⅓ tsp salt
1 ½ eggs, beaten
50 g pandan leaves, blended with 350 ml water, strained
a little green food colouring, if necessary

For the Filling
3 cups grated coconut flesh (about ¾ coconut)
90 g palm sugar (*gula Melaka*), chopped
3 tbsp water
1 pandan leaf, knotted
⅓ tsp salt
1 tsp cornflour, mixed with 1 tbsp water, for thickening

Method

To make the batter, sieve the flour and salt in a mixing bowl. Make a well in the centre and add the eggs, pandan fluid and colouring gradually, all the while mixing the flour into the water and slowly working from the centre outwards. When all is mixed, strain through a sieve to get a fine batter, and leave to stand for half an hour.

For the filling, heat the palm sugar and water in a saucepan until syrupy. Add the coconut, pandan leaf and salt, stirring all the while. Add the cornflour and water mix, and continue to cook until it thickens (approximately 12 minutes). Set aside to cool.

Heat a 15 cm/6 inch non-stick frying pan, grease with a little oil, then pour 1 scoop of batter into the pan; tilt it quickly to form a thin pancake. Cook on a low heat until set (approximately 6 minutes), then remove from the pan, place 1 tbsp filling on the pancake and roll up tightly like a *popiah*.

Repeat with the rest of the mixes, then place all on a serving plate and serve hot or cold as a snack or dessert.

Mango Soufflé

Sweet, intense and creamy, this summer pudding is redolent of the tropics. The scent and flavour of ripe mango predominates, while the texture is soft and light. For something refreshing on a hot day, this simple soufflé is hard to resist.

Serves 6
250 ml milk
2 tbsp vanilla essence
85 g fresh mango, puréed
80 g sugar
45 g flour
25 g butter
6 egg yolks

For the Meringue
6 egg whites
80 g sugar

Method

Put the milk, mango purée and vanilla essence into a saucepan, and bring to the boil. When the mix reaches boiling point, pour in the sugar and flour bit by bit and stir until the sugar dissolves and there are no lumps.

Remove from heat, set aside and allow to cool for approximately 2 to 3 minutes.

When the mix has cooled down, add the butter, stirring continuously until the butter combines with the mango mix. Repeat with the egg yolk, then allow to cool.

For the meringue, beat the egg whites and sugar until the mix forms into soft peaks, then fold in with the mango mix. It is best to use a spatula instead of a whisk for this, as this maintains the bubbles that help the soufflé to rise.

Spoon the mix into 6 separate ramekins or a mould that has been greased with butter, then bake in an oven set at 230°C for approximately 12 to 13 minutes, by which time the soufflé should have both risen and cooked through.

Serve with vanilla ice cream, if required.

Sucimurni *Smoothies*

Indelibly anchored in its milieu, Tanjong Jara Resort offers guests a totally authentic experience of real Malay life. Ninety percent of its staff comes from nearby villages with the aim of imparting the Malay philosophy of *sucimurni* to the guests. Roughly translated, this is a way of life that embraces purity of spirit, wellness and revitalisation.

A good way to embrace this is to whip up one of the resort's wholesome smoothies. Containing the freshest of local fruits and veggies — pineapples, oranges, cucumbers, bananas to name a few — along with roselle juice, they are tantalisingly tropical. Roselle is a type of red hibiscus (*Hibiscus sabdariffa L*) that was introduced to Malaysia from India and grows in profusion around the resort. Its juice has recently been manufactured and sold as a healthy concentrate, a little like the European cassis. High in Vitamin C and anthocyanins, it is easily made into a juice. Mix with water in a ratio of 1:8 or 1:10 depending on how sweet you want it.

Sucimurni Smoothie

Method

Blend the pineapple juice, cream and 15 ml of the roselle juice with the ice cubes, then pour into a glass. Pour the remaining roselle juice on top, so that it sinks to the bottom of the glass. Garnish with slices of pineapple — and serve immediately.

Ingredients
120 ml pineapple juice
dash of cream
30 ml roselle juice
8 ice cubes

Anjung

Method

Mix all in an electric blender and pour into a suitable glass. Garnish with a cucumber wheel and preserved roselle blossom — and serve immediately.

Ingredients
1 to 2 pieces cucumber
(depending on size)
30 ml roselle juice
8 ice cubes

Serambi

Method

Put all ingredients into an electric blender and mix, in interval mode, until thoroughly combined. Garnish with a hibiscus flower or preserved roselle blossom and pandan leaf — and serve immediately.

Ingredients
juice from 3 oranges,
freshly squeezed
30 ml roselle juice
8 ice cubes

One Island, One Resort

A holiday destination bar none, Pangkor Island Resort is a truly special place. Set on its own private island with a verdant jungle backdrop and an ocean on its doorstep, it combines luxurious pampering with outdoor activities. With overwater Malay-style villas on stilts, an innovative spa, plenty of water sports and its own resident naturalist, guests are encouraged to truly relax and revitalise amongst nature.

Of course, its culinary experiences are not to be missed either. After all, what could be more celebratory than eating in an intimate courtyard with plenty of pavilions for private dining, all the while watching chefs at work in any number of show kitchens? Called Feast Village, this is a popular option on the island, where a diverse array of dining options from the Asia Pacific region is on offer. There are also a bakery, a café and a wine cellar — so the whole experience is that of an up-market, open-air eatery with a unique take on the "moveable feast".

More than a restaurant, Feast Village can best be described as an exciting new interactive experience. Wannabe chefs take home top tips from the master chefs

ABOVE Open kitchens, dramatic décor with sumptuous materials and an array of tastes and odours characterise the sensory overload that is the Feast Village experience at Pangkor Laut Resort.

RIGHT Typical fare from the famous Malay Set.

in the various kitchens, then hone their skills in a cooking school where a variety of Asian dishes are taught in an informal setting. People watchers are kept entertained; and there's always something going on.

One of the main attractions is the Malay Set, a changing mélange of small dishes with a central rice staple. In the photo on the previous page we see a tomato rice dish, fringed with a delectable array of foods from both land and sea. Below, from left to right, spicy lamb masala; fish curry with lady's fingers; fried long beans; *daging masak kicap*, rich beef cubes cooked in soy sauce; and prawns with sambal sauce. As befits the Malaysian theme, culinary inspirations are from all corners of Asia — India, China and closer to home in southeast Asia.

BELOW A generous deck with marvellous sea views is an apt dining spot at Fisherman's Cove.

RIGHT A fine dining experience is offered with chefs in show kitchens serving up Asian fusion cuisine.

OPPOSITE Taking their cue from their natural surrounds, the overwater accommodations at the resort are based on Malay vernacular design.

Hook, Line and Sinker *Fisherman's Cove*

Dining at the edge of the sea in an al-fresco setting at Fisherman's Cove is a firm favourite of repeat guests to Pangkor Laut Resort. Sitting on the deck overlooking the sea, and eating fresh seafood is the order of the day — or evening — here. The chefs like to tailor-make the catch of the day to suit guests' tastes. They can go heavy on the spice, or make the dish plainer, lighter or more full flavoured — the habitual way of cooking in Malaysia, according to the head chef who hails from nearby Pangkor island.

Meat is flown in fresh from Australia; line fish and prawns come from Europe; and local fish is sourced from the fish market on Pangkor island. Expect such specialities as seaweed salad, pan-roasted local barramundi and tiger prawns in the savoury department and puddings with a flavour of the Orient — exotic caramelised Sarawak pineapple with a chocolate praline mousse is always popular.

Please turn overleaf to view our two Fisherman's Cove recipes.

Hot & Sour Venus Clam Soup

Ideally you should use daun selasih, a local Malay basil, to flavour this clam soup; it adds a sweet fragrancy to the dish which is characterised by tender, fresh clam meat and the aromas of the sea.

Serves 6

1.8 kg live Venus clams
80 g onion, finely sliced
15 g ginger, finely chopped
15 g garlic, finely chopped
1.4 litres full-bodied seafood stock
6 tomatoes
15 g *daun selasih* (local basil)
25 g tamarind paste
5 g dried chilli
salt and white pepper powder, to taste
fresh basil leaves, finely sliced
bird's eye chilli and a few drops of chilli oil, for garnish

Method

To prepare a tomato concasse, peel and seed the tomatoes, then chop finely. Set aside.

Sauté the garlic, ginger and sliced onion until fragrant, then add the clams. Remove all the clams once they open, then add the stock, tamarind, dried chilli and basil. Add salt and white pepper to taste.

Cover and simmer for 4 minutes, then strain.

Place the cooked clams in the middle of a warmed soup bowl with tomato concasse, basil leaves and chillies on top of the clams. Pour over the seasoned aromatic broth, drizzle with a few drops of chilli oil, and serve immediately.

Steamed Fillet of Saltwater Barramundi with Bird's Eye Chilli, Roasted Baby Eggplant & Pumpkin Sauce

Barramundi from the sea has a clean fish taste as compared to farmed barramundi, so this dish has a real fresh-from-the-ocean flavour. Baby eggplants are seedless, so they are easy to cook, and go well with the pumpkin sauce. Overall the sweetness of the pumpkin tones down the chillies, so this is not an overly spiced dish.

Serves 6

6 x 180 g fillets of saltwater barramundi
360 g baby eggplant (*nasu*)
90 g spicy sauce (see below)
90 g pumpkin sauce (see below)
sea salt and freshly ground white pepper, to taste
200 g pickled leeks
85 g salt
200 g tangerines, de-seeded and cut into pieces
750 ml chilli paste
350 ml spicy corn and dried chilli oil

for Spicy Sauce
420 g ginger flower
200 g lemongrass
250 g shallots
100 g garlic
50 g fresh turmeric
70 g bird's eye chillies

for Pumpkin Sauce
1 medium-sized pumpkin
600 ml chicken stock
1 star anise
1 cm cinnamon piece
4 cardamoms

green parsley, chopped, for garnish

Method

For the spicy sauce: Chop all the ingredients finely and season with salt. Put everything into a blender except the spicy oil and blend until a creamy consistency is achieved. Mix in the spicy corn and dried chilli oil at the end.

For the pumpkin sauce: Skin and seed the pumpkin, then chop into small pieces and boil in the chicken stock along with the spices for approximately 30 minutes. When the pumpkin is soft, remove all the spices and purée until creamy. Keep warm.

Steam the fish fillets in the spicy sauce for 6 minutes in *bain marie* style.

Cut the baby eggplant into 4 quarters and pan roast them with a lid on until they are soft and light brown in colour. This should take approximately 2 minutes.

Spoon the pumpkin sauce onto the centre of the plates and place the hot steamed fish fillet on top. Garnish with roasted *nasu* and a sprinkling of chopped green parsley and serve immediately.

Chapman's Bar Emerald Bay

Today, the peaceful beach and sea at Emerald Bay plays host to guests at Pangkor Laut Resort who enjoy a snooze in a hammock, a swim in crystal clear waters and a snack at its beach restaurant, Chapman's Bar. Tucking into a seafood salad or the Catch of the Day, they'd be forgiven for thinking this is one of the most peaceful spots on the planet. Its whisper-quiet, white-sand environs with gently lapping waves are disturbed by the odd seabird or monitor lizard — but that's about all these days.

It wasn't always so. During World War II, the horseshoe-shaped cove was the submarine pick-up and drop-off point for British army agents during the Japanese occupation of Malaya; it takes its name from the dramatic escape of one Colonel Frederick Spencer Chapman, DSO, in May 1945. Because of the depth of the waters

OPPOSITE AND BELOW An inviting beachside scene—lunch at Emerald Bay. Some of the summery fare at Chapman's Bar may include (from left to right): chicken and mushroom *tom yam* in young coconut; char-grilled lobster; Caesar salad folded with crispy French baguette; super-chilled fruit coulis in a half melon topped with mango sorbet. Mouthwatering!

Of the island's 300 acres, only a fraction has been developed to house Pangkor Laut Resort, the Spa Village and its eight Estates. Nature is respected here, almost revered; it rewards visitors in multiple ways.

and its location on the far side of the island, Emerald Bay was perfectly suited for clandestine submarine entries and departures in the dead of night.

Nearly 60 years later, Emerald Bay's tranquil waters are more likely to contain a sun worshipper, kayaker or swimmer than an undercover agent. For light refreshments, these holiday makers head for a deck chair or a beachside table in the shade of a sea almond tree and treat themselves to a light snack, cool fruit juice or delicious light lunch. Seafood is the highlight of the Chapman's Bar menu, along with traditional satay and salads, but there is also a delicious Sizzling Mongolian lamb barbecue, the recipe for which is overleaf. Try cooking it at home on a summer's day accompanied by a slightly chilled merlot.

Sizzling Mongolian Lamb

Rich demi-glaze gives a hearty flavour to this robust lamb dish whose origins lie on the steppes of Mongolia. If you can't experience it at Emerald Bay, make it for Sunday lunch.

Method

To make the sauce: In a heavy bottomed saucepan, melt the butter over a medium heat until it becomes frothy. Add the onions, carrots, celery and leeks, and sauté for a few minutes until slightly browned. Don't let them burn. With a wooden spoon, stir the flour into the mixture a little bit at a time until it is fully incorporated and forms a thick paste or roux. Lower the heat and cook the *roux* for another 5 minutes or so, until it turns light brown. Don't let it burn. Using a wire whisk, slowly add the stock and tomato purée, whisking vigorously to make sure it is free of lumps.

When fully incorporated and cooked, set aside 150 ml for this recipe.

Remove the excess fat from the top of lamb loin, and sear it on a hot grill or in a large frying pan for a few minutes.

Pound the Sichuan pepper pods, white peppercorns, mustard and coriander seeds in a large pestle until a fine powder is achieved, then rub the spice mix into the lamb loin. Fry in a heavy griddle pan or cook on a hot grill until medium rare (around 2 minutes). Set aside.

In another pan, sauté the onions and garlic until soft, then add the *demi-glaze* sauce and simmer for 8 minutes to achieve a not-too-thick sauce texture.

In another pan, sauté the leeks and carrots until they become soft (approximately 2 minutes).

To serve, slice the lamb on a hot plate, place together with the vegetables and pour the sauce on top. Serve immediately.

Serves 6
1.2 kg lamb loin
50 g Sichuan pepper pods
15 g white peppercorns
10 g mustard seeds
15 g coriander seeds
10 g sea salt
250 g leeks, sliced
250 g carrots, cut into oblongs
100 g onions, diced
40 g garlic, chopped
150 ml Demi-glaze Sauce (see below)

For the *Demi-glaze* Sauce (1 litre)
200 g onions, diced
200 g carrots, diced
150 g celery, diced
150 g leeks, diced
60 g clarified butter
50 g all-purpose flour
1.5 litres brown sauce
180 g tomato purée
a few bay leaves
couple of thyme sprigs

Eastern & Oriental Express

Voyage of Discovery

If exploring different cuisines and cultures is a passion, a trip on the Eastern & Oriental Express could be the answer to that holiday dilemma. Combining fine dining and exquisite service with luxury and attention to detail, a sojourn aboard the train's signature green-and-cream carriages is truly a voyage of discovery.

It has to be said that the word "express" is more than a bit of a misnomer, as any of the train trips that take in Singapore, Malaysia, Thailand and, more recently, Laos are hardly speedy. Rather, they offer a leisurely saunter through the Far East — allowing guests to soak up the varied and rich scenery from the comfort of the train. A number of outings punctuate the daily routine on board, which — thankfully for gourmets — is dominated by glorious cuisine.

Following in the footsteps of the famed Orient Express that has plied routes in Europe since 1883, the E & O (as it's fondly known) has been in operation since 1982. With a gleaming stainless-steel exterior and exquisitely panelled interiors

n elm, cherry, teak and rosewood, along with diamond-shaped marquetry, it is a oicture of elegance. Dining takes place in one of three restaurant cars: decked out n atmospheric lamplight, with brass overhead racks and specially designed china and crystalware, silver service is the norm. A bar in pale ash and a saloon carriage with a Chinese theme are suitably exotic, while everybody's favourite is the rear observation deck. Serviced by a small bar, it is the only carriage that is open air — t's perfect for sundowners as the train meanders through rubber or tea plantations, fields of emerald rice, or rolling hill country.

A number of different itineraries are available for the discerning traveller, but regardless of duration or location, each day begins with breakfast served on a tray n the cabin at a time specified by the guest: fresh pastries and croissants, steaming Cameron Highlands tea or coffee from Chiang Mai, fruit, cereals and juices. Believe me, you can very easily get used to breakfast in bed, E & O style! Comfy beds, n-room amenities, soft pillows — and an ever-changing panorama of Far Eastern countryside make for convivial companions.

Lunch and dinner are no less enticing: both are three-course affairs, served by extremely dexterous staff that somehow never spill a drop, despite the constant

ABOVE AND LEFT A dining car set up for service is elegance epitomised: The E & O signature is embossed on silverware, table napkins and accoutrements, giving a highly professional, not to mention beautiful, sheen at the dining table.

OPPOSITE All aboard! Guests are given personalised leather wallets, luggage tags and more before the start of their trip.

swaying of the train. How the chefs manage to produce such high-quality fare is a mystery: a tiny galley space where the team works cheek-by-jowel miraculously dishes out innovative East meets West cuisine — all using fresh, seasonal produce sourced locally. We are privileged to share two specials with you overleaf.

As if this were not enough, there are plenty of other diversions on board: a local astrologer, using a combination of Chinese zodiac techniques and palm reading, is a novelty, while a foot reflexology session in the library is deeply satisfying. And this is all without mention of convivial exchanges with fellow travellers — be sure to check out the bar for a post-prandial session of impromptu music with the resident pianist.

OPPOSITE, TOP LEFT & RIGHT Greet the new day with a laden breakfast tray in the comfort of your own train compartment.

OPPOSITE, BOTTOM LEFT Served as a sundowner, the exotic Shanghai Express cocktail teams bourbon, amaretto, orange and lime juice with grenadine syrup.

BELOW F & B is a large part of life aboard the train. Guests are encouraged to dress up in the evenings, with gentlemen "sure to be comfortable" in jacket and tie. Some delicacies, from left to right: Local Asian mushrooms are marinaded and presented along with a medley of seafood for a starter that is redolent of lemongrass; a classic chocolate tart with "coconut cloud" and raspberry coulis; a crunchy mix of gin and maraschino with lychee, lime, green apple and pineapple juices, this citrusy fresh cocktail is simply called the E & O; a hugely innovative combo of *tom yam* flavours and *vichyssoise* results in a creamy soup that is served with quail medallions and vegetable tagliatelle — a firm favourite amongst the team.

BOTTOM From left to right: Gold-and-burgundy tones add glamour to the library; a corner in the bar where salted nuts and pre-dinner snacks await a guest; lighting greatly contributes to the overall feel of the carriages; an elegant silver coffee pot and dessert is set beside a classic floral arrangement for a guest.

Medallion of Beef with Foie Gras Croquette, Asian Vegetables, Vindaloo Sauce and Mustard Foam

Combining tastes from East and West, this tenderloin dish (preferably cooked rare or medium-rare), is accompanied by a flavoursome, but not too spicy, Vindaloo sauce that uses a whole gamut of southeast Asian spices. The light croquette with goose liver is a crunchy, yet satisfying, companion.

Method

Prepare the vegetables, then blanch in salted boiling water until cooked *al dente*; remove and place in a bowl of iced water.

Mix all the Vindaloo sauce spices. Set aside.

For the croquettes: Peel and boil the potatoes in salted water. Remove and mash. Add flour, milk, eggs, butter and nutmeg, then continue mashing the mixture until it is smooth and creamy.

Season the duck liver slices with salt and pepper before searing on a very high heat, 1 minute on each side, until a crisp surface is formed.

Take some mashed potato mix and a slice of cooked liver and form into a ball. Repeat five times. Place the balls in the freezer for about 30 minutes. When the balls are hard, remove, roll in a bit more flour and the breadcrumbs and deep fry in oil for 1 minute, then finish in the oven at 180ºC for 3 minutes.

For the steaks: Season with salt and pepper, and cook over a high heat until done. Remove, deglaze the pan with red wine and reduce by half. Add the Vindaloo spices and beef stock, then continue to reduce for a further 5 minutes.

To finish, sauté the vegetables in butter, then arrange in the middle of a plate. Top with the beef medallion and gently pour the Vindaloo sauce over. Crown with the croquette, garnish with a sprig of chervil, and serve.

Serves 6

1.1 kg beef tenderloin (cut into 6 steaks of 180 g each)
5 ml oil
10 g butter
200 ml beef stock
50 ml red wine
150 g green peas
200 g snow peas
200 g soya beans

For the Foie Gras Croquette

400 g potatoes
200 g duck liver, sliced
160 g breadcrumbs
150 g plain flour
120 ml milk
2 eggs
10 g butter
pinch nutmeg, grated
salt and pepper, to taste

For the Vindaloo Sauce

2 tsp cumin, ground
1 tsp chilli powder
2 tsp black mustard seeds
1 ½ tsp cinnamon, ground
80 ml white wine vinegar
1 tsp salt
1 tsp sugar
1 tsp cardamom, ground
2 tsp turmeric, ground
½ tsp cloves, ground
1 tsp cracked black pepper
3 cloves garlic, crushed
1 ½ tsp ginger, crushed

Goose Liver and Vegetables in Chinese Cabbage with Pumpkin and Coconut Velouté

Serves 6
1 long Chinese cabbage
150 g oyster mushrooms
150 g beansprouts
80 g pickled ginger
150 g duck confit, shredded
180 g goose liver (in 6 x 30 g pieces)
70 ml duck fat
salt and pepper, to taste

For the Velouté
1 kg pumpkin, chopped into pieces
400 g white onion, sliced
400 g leeks, sliced
2 stalks lemongrass, crushed
3 lime leaves, crushed
60 g blue ginger, crushed
1 litre chicken stock
500 ml coconut milk
6 bacon strips, cooked until crispy

A fusion of occidental and oriental ingredients, this brightly coloured soup is creamy, flavoursome and fulsome. The central "ball" is a cabbage and foie gras layered concoction: surprisingly robust, it adds texture (and taste, of course) to the creamy velouté.

Method

For the cabbage and goose liver: Clean 6 cabbage leaves to be used for wrapping. Julienne the balance of the cabbage, then sauté with duck fat, mushrooms and beansprouts. Set aside.

Bring a large pot of salted water to the boil, and blanch the 6 cabbage leaves. Remove, cool and pat dry.

Lay one cabbage leaf on a piece of cling film, place one piece of goose liver in the middle of the leaf and top with a small pile of the sautéed ingredients, duck confit and pickled ginger. Fold in the edges of the leaf, wrap into a round parcel, then gather up the edges of the cling film to seal tightly. Steam parcels for 5 to 10 minutes. Set aside.

For the soup: Sauté the pumpkin flesh, onions and leeks, then add chicken stock, lemongrass, lime leaves and ginger and boil until cooked. Remove from heat and leave for 10 minutes. Remove the ginger, lemongrass and lime leaves, then blend the mixture until fine. Bring to the boil once again, then infuse with coconut milk.

To serve, remove the cling film from the cabbage and goose liver parcels, then place folded side down in shallow soup plates. Top with a cripsy bacon strip. Gently and evenly pour the velouté to surround the parcel and finish with a drizzle of coconut milk. Garnish with rocket sprigs, if desired.

RIGHT AND BELOW Afternoon tea is served in the Jim Thompson Tea Lounge at the Cameron Highlands Resort; delicacies include fresh strawberries, cookies, cakes and scones.

OPPOSITE Tea and cakes are served in the privacy of one's own tea garden — in a secluded spot with spectacular views over lush valleys below.

English Tea Celebrating an Institution

Even though the Chinese were credited with discovering tea, it is the English who have made the art of drinking tea their own. There is nothing more quintessentially English than a pot of tea at 4pm — served with sandwiches, cakes and scones along with strawberry jam and clotted cream, of course.

We celebrate this ritual at a number of different locations: in a colonial outpost in Malaysia's Cameron Highlands; at two locations in downtown Kuala Lumpur; and at an English country cottage in Berkshire. Somehow the act of brewing and pouring this amber liquid from pot to cup, adding milk and sugar as required, stirring and sipping has brought comfort across continents for centuries. It has not been called a genteel meal for nothing.

CAMERON HIGHLANDS RESORT

The British colonial hill station is as good a place as any to start: Spanning across the empire, more often than not such outposts resembled mini recreations of Surrey or Sussex villages transplanted to the tropics. The Cameron Highlands, situated on a 1,500m high plateau in mountainous forestland running along the borders of Pahang and Perak states, was no exception. Today, at the Cameron Highlands Resort, a boutique hideaway with a nostalgic air, guests can partake of an intimate afternoon tea in the middle of a nearby tea plantation. Included in the bespoke experience is a visit to the BOH tea factory, a walk around its plantation, and a tea-tasting session, all culminating in a picnic beneath an umbrella in the midst of rolling, velvety tea gardens. There's also "normal" afternoon tea in the resort's cosy lounge by the roaring fire to take into consideration. In addition to scones and cakes, you're bound to be presented with a bowl of freshly plucked strawberries: the area's fertile slopes, cool climate and plentiful rainfall are perfect for growing temperate specials, strawberries and roses being just two examples. Even though the sun may have set on the British Empire, its tradition of tea at 4pm continues unabated.

STARHILL TEA SALON

Back in the metropolitan surrounds of Jalan Bukit Bintang in Kuala Lumpur, there are two terrific afternoon tea options: The Lobby Lounge at the up-market Ritz-Carlton and the Starhill Tea Salon in Starhill Gallery. The latter is a free-form space set amongst columns of stacked tea tins in pastel shades, with golden lights made from tea tins above and luxe seating clusters in burgundy and browns below. Silk and velvet cushions, swirling patterns, and the crooning of jazz from concealed speakers give a suitably luxe feel — it's the perfect spot to rest tired toes after a shopping extravaganza.

Open daily from 10am to 1am, there are over 60 different assorted teas to choose from, along with French pastries, freshly baked scones, preserves and clotted cream, iced cream sundaes, and assorted sandwiches. In the evening the atmosphere becomes a bit buzzy with post-prandial cigars, cocktails and a selection of desserts for the after dinner crowd.

For something refined, with the strains of the resident harpist as an accompaniment, you could try the clubby Lobby Lounge at The Ritz-Carlton across the bridge. Decked out with leather sofas, classic paintings, an antique dresser of crockery, pannelled walls and a dark bar, it offers intimate clusters of tables and chairs — the perfect spot for a clandestine *rendez-vous à deux* or a pre-dinner whisky and cigar. The main event, however, is the traditional English afternoon tea: naturally freshly-baked scones with clotted cream and strawberry jam are *de rigeur*, but there's also a selection of pies, puffs, sandwiches and cakes.

LEFT The design at the Starhill Tea Salon is luxe, contemporary, and cute. Tea tin columns in pastels are the main event.

BELOW Silver service to the strains of the hotel's resident harpist ... the tea experience at The Ritz-Carlton is deluxe and decadent.

LOBBY LOUNGE, THE RITZ-CARLTON

BRAY HOUSE

In the words of an 8th-century Chinese poet: "Tea tempers the spirit, harmonises the mind, dispels lassitude and relieves fatigue, awakens thought and prevents drowsiness."

LEFT A table groaning with crumpets, scones, sandwiches and cakes—small and large—is set for English tea on a gorgeous spring day in an English garden in Bray. What could be a more agreeable way to while away an hour or two?

ABOVE Bray-on-Thames not only has the river Thames running alongside its Tudor-style cottages, but many smaller tributaries also. Many of these have adjacent foot-paths, excellent for a post-tea stroll.

But, really, there's no better place than home for that afternoon cuppa. At Bray House, a country idyll on the River Thames in the UK, that's exactly what you get — all the trappings of a home. There's the sweet patio garden, the village atmosphere, a comfy living room, and plenty of delicious tea items prepared by your own private in-house chef — what could be more satisfying than a cup of Earl Grey or *lapsang souchong* to accompany all that?

The Quintessential English

Country Village

BELOW AND OPPOSITE The architecture at Bray dates back to Tudor times, with pretty streets containing rows of timber-framed cottages, many with narrow windows and steeply pitched roofs.

ABOVE A detail on the side of St Michael's church in Bray. The large church was built in the early 1300s to replace a previous Saxon building, destroyed in 1294.

Situated on the banks of the river Thames, surrounded by typically English green and rolling countryside, sits the idyllic village of Bray-on-Thames. Part of the area that was once home to the vast Windsor forest, the earliest buildings date back to the 14th century. Today's celebrity residents, Michael Parkinson and Heston Blumenthal amongst them, keep its allure alive; but in the past notable inhabitants have included King Charles II, Nell Gwynn and Thomas Hughes.

Today, as in earlier times, Bray comprises a cluster of Tudor-beamed cottages with low ceilings and tiled roofs, with some larger villas and estates fronting the Thames. Swathes of green lawn and clusters of weeping willows, their elegantly curving fronds sweeping across fast-flowing waters, line the river; swans, Canadian geese and ducks bob up and down; and hedgerows and verges are full of wild flowers in spring. As far as its buildings go, the handsome church of St Michael dating back to Norman times is worth a visit.

There are plenty of bridleways and walks, horse riding is a popular pastime, while a trip up or down the river messing around with the locks is a wonderful way to while away a summer's day. Other nearby attractions include the town of Henley-on-Thames, the race track at Royal Ascot, a visit to Windsor Castle or Eton College, and the magnificent country estate of Cliveden.

Most recently, however, Bray has become well known amongst foodies: housing two of the nation's four three-Michelin-star restaurants, as well as a couple of excellent gastro-pubs and more, it attracts gourmands from all over the world.

RIVER COTTAGE

To Let

First up in Bray was the Waterside Inn, a "restaurant with rooms" opened in 1972 by the legendary Roux brothers of Le Gavroche fame. Forty years on, it is still family owned and run, today's patron being one of the sons, Alain Roux. With a three Michelin star standing, a formidable reputation and a welcoming, informal atmosphere, it continues to serve inspirational French cuisine in attractive riverside surrounds.

More recently, Bray has generated kilometres of copy through the culinary experiments of Heston Blumenthal, one of the world's leading exponents of a new

ABOVE The Crown serves tasty British pub food with carefully sourced seasonal ingredients in a cosy 16th-century interior. Here, we see a photogenic starter, main course and pudding: from left to right, Rhubarb Eton Mess, Pork Pie and Picalili, Battered Fish with Crushed Peas and Chips — all updated versions of traditional British staples.

OPPOSITE Signs for eateries include one for the Hind's Head (exterior seen on right) and The Fat Duck.

type of cooking that, in his words, embraces "excellence, openess and integrity". Since this self-taught chef opened The Fat Duck in 1995, it has garnered more awards than I care to list along with a hefty dose of controversy, as Blumenthal tries to re-educate his clientele in the art of eating. Put it like this: if combos like cauliflour and chocolate intrigue you and you have deep pockets, check it out.

For those who can't dig deep enough, but are interested all the same, Blumenthal's finesse may be savoured at two traditional inns round the corner — the Hind's Head and the Crown. The former specialises in traditional British

dishes and seasonal ingredients: its elegant, slightly severe interiors are housed in a hostelry that dates from Tudor times — and many of the dishes have been created with the help of food historians at nearby Hampton Court Palace. There are very traditional British items such as Scotch Eggs, Oxtail and Kidney Pudding, and more.

Otherwise, there is the Caldesi in Campagna, a swanky Italian, or Michael Parkinson's nearby pub, the Royal Oak, which also boasts one Michelin star. Quite how this little village came to house so many first-rate restaurants is a bit of a mystery — but house it they do!

A Home away from Home

If a trip to the gourmet haven of Bray is on your list of must-dos, we cannot recommend highly enough the concierge service provided by Private Label and the cosy three-bedroom Bray House. Set on the main street, it retains its English cottage façade, but has been extensively renovated and upgraded to provide an upscale English country house experience. What was once the stable block to Bray Manor is now a traditional home, but with a unique, contemporary twist in the décor.

ABOVE Bray House's pretty façade with geraniums in window boxes (left) and breakfast laid out in the cool courtyard (right).

OPPOSITE TOP English breakfast in the sweet patio garden consists of bacon and eggs, tomatoes, mushrooms, along with toast and preserves, juice and coffee.

OPPOSITE BOTTOM Bray House, on the extreme left, lies adjacent to the Hind's Head public house.

All modern conveniences are enclosed within its atmospheric walls: a super kitchen, fabulous rain showers, wi-fi, music and TV system, art-deco bar, open fireplace ready laid for lighting, and more. Candles are lit on arrival; all the items you need for breakfast are thoughtfully laid out in the fridge; and your hosts (who live nearby) organise trips and make bookings for you as required. Small touches, such as daily newspapers or cappuccinos from nearby Maidenhead brought to your door, are unbeatable.

The English country house experience has been updated at Bray House: Outdated décor and outmoded plumbing have been replaced by first-class service and top-notch amenities, yet the warm, inviting atmosphere of old remains.

CLOCKWISE FROM TOP LEFT Everything at Bray House, both design wise and in terms of conveniences and produce, is designed to indulge. Beautiful tub in the master suite beneath the eaves; stable doors lead from kitchen/diner to courtyard; bacon and eggs laid out for breakfast in the courtyard; an all-white bedroom with romantic four-poster; the individual bar.

OVERLEAF A fresh picnic and boat trip along the Thames is part of the bespoke experience at Bray House.

You'll be left alone to rise at the time of your liking, and since all the items for a traditional British fry-up are thoughtfully provided, it's up to you whether you opt or the full Monty or go for cereals, fruits and Duchy Originals creamy yoghurts. Lunch and afternoon tea are at your discretion, and in the evening, after you've over-imbibed at one of the local restaurants, there's nothing more luxurious than strolling home to a beautifully romantic turn-down — complete with candles, roses and your choice of soft music.

RIGHT AND BELOW Potatoes and sweetcorn are two of Hokkaido's specialities: grilled or steamed, they are eaten year round. It is apparently the white kernels that give the corns their exceptional sweetness.

OPPOSITE Cured meats — ham, sausage, marinated beef — along with oysters and fish from Otaru are prepared outdoors Hokkaido-style.

Niseko Fresh Food and Fresh Powder ... Daily

Niseko, on the island of Hokkaido, has hit international headlines for its powder skiing, but it is equally well known amongst foodies for its seasonal farm produce: delicious carrots, asparagus and potatoes grow well in the island's fertile volcanic soils aided by the extreme variants between day and night temperatures. Exceptionally sweet corn on the cob, grilled on open fires, is another speciality. Try the "morning picked corn" or *asamogi tokibi* which tastes very different when picked before sunrise rather than after.

Another item said to to be better picked ripe and early is the Yotei melon, the perfect accompaniment to some of the areas's locally cured hams. In addition to these hams, there are specialist sausages — or try the bacon or mutton barbecue.

The Shiribetsu river has plentiful stocks of rainbow trout, red-spotted *masu* salmon and Japanese char, while crustaceans are prized for their size and value. And of course there is the bounty from the oceans: Hokkaido scallops, snow crabs

OPPOSITE Wintry fare: The deck adjacent to The Green Leaf Niseko Village's restaurant is ideal for barbecues; regional fare includes Hokkaido scallops, snow crabs and fish, fresh from the market at nearby Otaru.

and other cold-water fish are world famous. When cooked at Niseko they have the added bonus of being super fresh.

The Green Leaf Niseko Village, a contemporary ski lodge that merges modernism with alpine flourishes and some Japanese touches, boasts an outdoor deck complete with gondola cabin seating, a fire pit and open barbecue. Drink in spectacular views over Mount Yotei, a 1,898 m dormant volcano that dominates the landscape, while imbibing a local Hokkaido beer and a seasonal barbecue.

BELOW, RIGHT AND OPPOSITE
Japan's islands are surrounded by cold-water oceans, so seafood is an important ingredient in Japanese cuisine. Within Hokkaido prefecture, *uni* (sea urchin), scallops, crabs, *ikura* (salmon roe), prawns, as well as a variety of seaweeds and fish, are highly prized.

Other spots include the hotel restaurant which is known as Goskhiki. Translating as "five different colours" in Japanese, Goshiki features a colourful fusion of Japanese, Asian and Western dishes that utilise fresh fish from both sea and freshwater lakes and rivers and the region's famous vegetables. In the winter, warming *nabe* hot pot dishes with Shiroishi beef and Makkari pork, all-you-can-eat snow crab-legs and grilled rockfish seasoned with *saikyo miso*, and a variety of *ramen* dishes are popular items in a restaurant that sports a striking open kitchen and gorgeous views over nearby ski slopes.

Local food and regional customs mean a lot to the Japanese: During the winter, people travel to Hokkaido's coastal seaports to sample crab; in the summer, giving boxes of fresh fruit to family and friends is an annual custom. This ensures that even city folk are attuned to the rhythms of agriculture and the countryside.

HILTON NISEKO VILLAGE

With celebrated interiors, and more than eight restaurants to choose from, Hilton Niseko Village offers a selection of casual and formal dining venues.

FAR LEFT Flame: the bar (above) and a sensational hanging fire-place (below) are surrounded by seating clusters in scarlet.

LEFT A screened off seating area in the hotel's Japanese restaurant.

ABOVE Only the finest quality beef, seafood and seasonal vegetables are prepared in front of your eyes at Pirka, the teppanyaki restaurant.

Another alternative for fresh seasonal fare is the Hilton Niseko Village, a hotel with ski-in and gondola-out facilities. The head chef here is an aficionado of both Japanese cuisine and the Japanese language: his intention is to always showcase both Hokkaido's and the country's unique culinary heritage.

Boasting a number of different eating venues and sharing two recipes with us (overleaf), the hotel's kitchens consistently innovate with whatever speciality is in season. The teppanyaki counter at Pirka (above) is a must for those who like to observe precision cutting and cooking, and follow this with some consuming of their own. Only the finest quality beef, seafood and local vegetables are used; there are also some innovative combinations such as reindeer and foie gras. For fresh seafood chowder or something more casual, Flame (far left) with its unusual central fire feature is a favourite, while a variety of other venues are always popular.

Herb Grilled Hokkaido Scallop and Tuna Tataki with Seasonal Vegetable Salad

This locally inspired dish utilizes fresh seafood from Nemuro, a town on the northeast coast of Hokkaido where the scallops are known for both their large size and their succulence. The ginger dressing is light so doesn't detract from the seafood, while the veggies are simply a suggestion; if in doubt, choose seasonal fare wherever possible.

Serves 6
6 scallops (40 g each)
120 g tuna
30 g Herb Butter (see below)
60 ml Ginger Dressing (see right)
10 ml light olive oil
30 g carrots
6 sugar snap peas
6 baby tomatoes
¼ zucchini
6 *okura* (lady's fingers)

For the Herb Butter
225 g unsalted butter
15 g parsley
a handful chervil
a handful Italian parsley
3 g salt
12 g garlic, crushed

For the Ginger Dressing
100 g onion, grated
80 g carrot, grated
9 g sugar
60 ml soya sauce
170 ml salad oil
4 g salt
80 ml vinegar
20 g ginger, grated

For the Tuna Tataki Marinade
90 ml soy
90 ml mirin
90 ml sake

Method

To make the herb butter: Take the butter out of the fridge and keep at room temperature until soft. Put all the ingredients in a food processer and mix well. Wrap the butter in cling film, form a long sausage shape about 3.5 cm thick and place in the fridge until needed.

For the marinade: Mix the three ingredients, then put tuna in the marinade for 30 minutes. Remove from marinade and dry well with kitchen paper. Sear the surface of the tuna in a hot frying pan briefly (about 2 to 3 minutes), then plunge into iced water to cool down; dry well with kitchen paper. With a sharp knife slice the tuna into 5 mm thick slices; set aside.

To make the ginger dressing: Put all ingredients in a bowl and whisk together. Keep in the fridge until needed.

Wash the scallops well in cold water and dry on kitchen paper.

Cut the vegetables into bite-sized pieces and blanch briefly in boiling water, then arrange the cooked vegetables on the plates.

Sauté the scallops in the light olive oil until cooked through (about 3 to 4 minutes). Place the scallops on the plates beside the vegetables. Melt 30 g of garlic butter and pour some over each scallop. Dress the vegetables with the ginger dressing and serve immediately.

Grilled Makkari Herb Pork with Wafu Sauce

A farm at Makkari, near Niseko, specialises in rearing pigs. Not any old pigs, you understand, but somewhat pampered pigs who, from 180 days old until their culling, are fed a herbal diet of ginger, oregano, nutmeg and cinnamon along with fresh Yotei spring water full of minerals. This apparently sweetens the fat and takes away the gamey smell, but ordinary pork is fine too.

Serves 6
6 pork loins (100g each)
15 ml light olive oil
60 g *daikon* (Japanese radish), grated
180 g Wafu Sauce (see below)
30 g carrots, cut into bite-sized pieces
60 g potatoes, cut into bite-sized pieces
60 g broccoli, cut into bite-sized pieces

For the Wafu Sauce
110 ml chicken stock
110 ml soy sauce
50 ml mirin
10 g sugar
30 g onion, chopped
¼ apple, chopped
5 g garlic, crushed
8 g ginger, crushed
5 g honey

Method

Blend all the sauce ingredients in a blender until a purée consistency is achieved. Transfer to a saucepan and bring to a simmer. Remove from the heat; set aside.

Sauté the pork in a hot frying pan with the olive oil or brush with the oil and cook on a grill for about 3 to 4 minutes on each side. If it is a thick chop, the pork may need a little longer.

Grill or sauté the vegetables, then arrange on a plate with the pork loin. Warm the sauce, add the grated *daikon* and pour over the pork. Serve immediately.

ABOVE The Green Leaf *onsen* excels as one of the most outstanding natural rock pools in Niseko. With separate indoor and outdoor pools for men and women, guests are encouraged to "take the waters" in the sodium-rich baths. The water emerges from the ground at 53°C and is cooled to just over 40°C before it enters the baths.

In addition to the powder snow, Niseko's volcanic geology results in an abundance of hot springs (*onsen*) that range from simple stone baths to vast luxurious pools. One of the best views to Mt Yotei is from the sodium-rich waters of the Hilton Niseko Village's indoor/outdoor *onsen*, while The Green Leaf Niseko Village's more intimate baths are very pretty. Sitting in a snowy landscape, with hot, mineral-rich waters soothing muscles over-worked from a day on the slopes is very therapeutic.

In Japan, it is traditional to take the waters at an *onsen*, then retire to a small guesthouse or *ryokan* where you're served some local specialities. The team at the Hilton were kind enough to share some of their *chinmi* — small snacks that are often served at such establishments along with sake or *shochu* (see overleaf). The snacks are generally salty, so also go well with beer.

Slices of local dried salmon called *sake toba* (*sake* is "salmon", *toba* is the type of drying method) are a little chewy, but perfectly balanced with mirin, spices and salt (below right). The same can be said for the selection of pickles: specifically mountain yam pickled with natural spring water, dark soy sauce, mirin, vinegar and bonito flakes; cucumber with mustard, shoyu, sugar and salt, turnip with red perilla leaf and salt; as well as little helpings of pickled burdock and eggplant (second from right).

BELOW *Chinmi* literally translates as "rare taste", but really refers to regional snacks that are delicacies. Most involve pickled items and seafood.

If *edamame* are your thing, be sure to try Hokkaido *edamame* (above left), as farmers swear they are the best in the country during the summer months! And, naturally, slices of bean curd with horseradish (above far left) are full of all the amino acids that the body needs: Japanese cuisine's reputation as being one of the healthiest in the world isn't a myth. What could be better than eating a satisfying and tasty meal — and knowing it's doing you the world of good as well?

Centuries of Tradition *Sake and Shochu*

*S**ake*, a rice-based alcoholic drink, permeates through all aspects of Japanese culture — from religious ceremonies to family celebrations. It's over 2,000 years old and is often called rice wine, though it is more like beer in its brewing process as it is produced through multiple levels of fermentation. It's made from a particular type of rice, and varies wildly in quality. *Sake* can be drunk hot or cold though the best *sakes* are served very cold.

The first step is the polishing of the rice to remove the outer bran; the more it is polished and the more the inner section of the grain is brought out, the better the *sake*. It is then exposed to *koji* mould (*Aspergillus oryzae*) to break down the starch into sugars, then *shubo* or yeast mash is added to kickstart a secondary fermentation. The final step is the addition of yeast — this turns these sugars into the liquid known as *sake*.

Other quality factors include the variety of mould used in fermentation, the chemical composition of the spring water used, and the type of fermentation processes employed. Certainly, to the unitiated, it's a specialist field that newcomers

OPPOSITE Traditionally, *sake* barrels, called *komodaru* (after the word *komo*, which is "woven straw") are covered with caligraphy-printed wrapping and tied with rope.

ABOVE *Sake* and *shochu* bottles come in many different sizes and designs: in the past the drink was often served in a wooden box measuring cup, known as a *masu* which has a volume of 180 ml. This tradition continues today, but glass and ceramic cups are also popular.

can be forgiven for stumbling at. Suffice it to say, we're not going to go into the thousands of different permutations on the subject: we're just giving you some basic info and some pretty pictures — and leaving you to do the experimentation!

Another Japanese alcoholic beverage is *shochu*, a liquor distilled from barley, wheat or other agricultural produce. In Hokkaido, a very particular *shochu* made from the area's famous sweet potatoes is valued for its strong taste and distinctive smell — but, as with *sake*, there are infinite varieties and qualities. In general, *shochu* is made in warmer temperatures, so is more widespread and popular in western and southern Japan. In Kagoshima prefecture, for example, no sake is produced, only the sweet, pungent local yam *shochu*.

Our recommendation? Ask the barman, and keep an open mind!

OPPOSITE A selection of delicacies from the kitchen at the Jamu Bar showcase how Japanese cuisine can be healthy, yet still tasty.

BELOW Vistas from the open-to-the-elements Jamu Bar take in the swimming pool, verdant greenery and some of the spa's reflecting pools and steps.

Healing through Health — *Japanese Style*

The Spa Village at Pangkor Laut Resort is a homage to nature within a quiet, secluded jungle-and-sea environment. The perfect place to shut out worldly concerns and seek inner peace, it is not just about therapies: it's more of a holistic journey — all the programs include inner and outer beauty therapies, cleansing, spiritual awakening and more.

A large part of any health retreat is food — or lack of food. Many people check in for a week or so at Spa Village in oder to lose weight, detox, clear the system, and generally rest and recharge. Therapists and doctors, be they pan-Asian, Ayurvedic, TCM (Traditional Chinese Medicine) or other all work on the premise that the body needs sustenance during times of stress. As a result the Jamu Bar, set in a tranquil spot overlooking the Straits of Malacca, offers a wonderful selection of healthy dishes, many of them Japanese or Japanese-inspired.

In general, the Japanese diet is low in fat, high in carbs and protein and it uses foods that are rich in nutrients and antioxidants. Sushi and sashimi, both served at the Jamu Bar, are brimming with vitamin A and omega-3 fatty acids, perfect protection against various types of cancer. Another favourite is natural soy products like tofu and *edamame* (green soyabeans); both are low in saturated fats and rich in calcium. The same can be said for the array of veggies — bamboo shoots, burdock

Chinese cabbage, corn, *daikon* radish, eggplant, shiitake mushrooms, soybeans, sweet potato and seaweeds — all used liberally at the Jamu Bar. The latter, in particular, are rich in antioxidants and minerals.

A week luxuriating in an overwater villa, taking in a variety of spa treatments and dining in style on soups, salads, raw fish and other Japanese dishes is many people's idea of heaven. Take a private dining table by the sea in the evening: with the jungle as backdrop, the lapping waves as a tableau in front, and delicious Japanese cuisine on your plate, you'll find your stress levels decreasing rapidly.

A Taste of Japan in *Kuala Lumpur*

In Japan, the aesthetic of what something looks like is often as important as the actual item itself. This particularity is exemplified at Gonbei San, an award-winning restaurant in Starhill Gallery in Kuala Lumpur, where the design of the restaurant more than matches the quality of the food.

Conceptualised by Yuhkichi Kawai of Design Spirits, the multi-space restaurant houses five sections, each with a separate counter offering *teppanyaki*, *sushi*, *robatayaki*, *tempura* and *sake*. Areas are separated by partitions of stacked green bottles and blue-and-white ceramic bowls: There's a semi-private sunken seating space backed by a wall of assorted *tenugui*, cotton hand towels that were popular 300 years ago as kabuki actors used them as name cards; another section sports heavy rustic-style furniture with a wall of *kamon* or traditional Japanese family crests; some may prefer the sake counter where dark chairs look over the bar on to a sea of sake barrels.

Wherever you choose to sit, you'll be attended to thoughtfully by members of staff that truly cherish the menu. The chefs fly in many items fresh from Japan and source seasonal specialities locally; they believe that authenticity is key. Signature dishes include Kobe beef *teriyaki*, fish steamed with rice wine, and *sake kasu udon*

GONBEI SAN

OPPOSITE MIDDLE At the tempura counter, pots are suspended from ornately carved fish hooks over a charcoal fire.

TOP A stacked ceramic "wall" shelters an area with low seating.

ABOVE An eye-catching arched bamboo tunnel leads into the restaurant, while stacked bottle "walls" delineate areas within.

or *soba*, a soupy noodle dish cooked with rice wine and accompanied with fresh veggies and seafood.

The two recipes Gonbei San shares with us (overleaf) are a soft shell crab maki roll that the head chef invented over 20 years ago and an oyster starter where the oysters are cooked in their shells with salty roe and sweet mayonnaise. Both make a great entrée for what will come after.

Soft Shell Crab Maki

Soft shell crabs add an interesting texture to this maki roll; with crunchy legs and crispy body, they are one of life's culinary delights. Add to them the mild smoky/salty taste of tobiko roe and the very Japanese Kewpie mayonnaise — and you have an authentic maki roll that isn't too difficult to make.

Serves 6
900 g soft shell crab
1.5 kg sushi rice, cooked
6 sheets seaweed, each 18 cm x 18 cm
180 g *tobiko* (flying fish roe)
120 g *kyuri* (Japanese pickled cucumber)
60 g Kewpie mayonnaise 3 l soy bean oil
dusting flour

for Sushi Rice Vinegar
320 ml *mizukan shiragiku* vinegar
180 g sugar
pinch salt

For the Soft Shell Crab Marinade
540 ml water
20 g salt
20 g bonito flakes (*hon dashi*)
1 egg

Method

First, mix all ingredients for the marinade, and marinate the soft shell crab in it for 30 minutes.

Mix the sushi rice vinegar ingredients together, then mix with the cooked sushi rice.

Pat dry the water on the surface of the marinated soft shell crab and dip it into the flour all over, then deep fry the soft shell crab in soy bean oil.

Place a sheet of seaweed onto a bamboo sushi rolling mat and spread 250 g of sushi rice on it. Top with 10 g of Kewpie mayonnaise and place 30 g of flying fish roe on top. Sprinkle 20 g of cucumber and the fried soft shell crab on top, then roll it up. Once successfully rolled up, cut the *maki* into 8 pieces.

Repeat with the next 5 sheets.

Serve with wasabi, sushi ginger and soy sauce.

Kaki Agebonoyaki

In Japanese "kaki" translates as "oyster" and "agebonoyaki" is a type of grilling that includes the shell. If you are an oyster fan, these little gems will tempt and tantalise: the overall sensation is of soft oyster, with a salty tang from the roe and a sweetness from the mayonnaise. They should be eaten immediately after cooking.

Serves 6

24 oysters (approx 25 g each)
dusting plain flour
black pepper, to taste
480 g Kewpie mayonnaise
60 g *mentaiko* (cod fish roe)
20 g sugar
70 g *lollo rosso* lettuce (a type of loose-leaf red lettuce)
70 g green coral lettuce
50 g cherry tomatoes
30 g onion rings
70 g thousand island dressing

Method

Mix the Kewpie mayonnaise, *mentaiko* and sugar thoroughly. Set aside.

Remove the oysters from their shells, dip into the flour on both sides and pan fry them. Add some pepper to the oysters during the pan frying.

Heat up the oyster shells in the oven until warm.

Place the fried oysters on the warm oyster shells neatly and spread the *mentaiko* mayonnaise on the oysters.

Bake the oysters in an oven set at 250°C until the oysters turn a golden-yellowish color. This should take about 1 minute.

Mix the lettuces, tomatoes and onion rings together with the thousand island dressing, and serve the oysters with this as a side salad.

LEFT Elegant signage is part and parcel of the whole experience of dining at Shook!.

RIGHT Seating clusters surround the *teppanyaki* counter, so guests can observe the chefs at work. Smell and sound are also part of the multi-sensory experience.

Shook! in Kuala Lumpur is a stylish, modern, open-concept restaurant that offers fine dining in salubrious surrounds. It's buzzy, busy, a real people watcher's place. It also has four show kitchens — Japanese, Chinese Wok, Italian and Western Grill — so there's always something to look at and listen to: a chef chopping, a stir-fry sizzling, a bottle of champagne popping.

In addition, there's usually a bit of a fanfare as you enter and take your seat: the waiters welcome you with traditional greetings, a little bell rings ... or is that my imagination? In any case, it's convivial and friendly, as well as comfortable, spacious and cool. An added bonus is that the waiters are extremely well-informed about the food.

Shook! opened in December 1999 and quickly gained prominence as an exciting restaurant concept and the first of its kind in Malaysia. Following seasonal trends, it boasts an adventurous menu that takes the best from East and West. There's a selection of Japanese, Chinese, Italian and Western cuisines, but we're concentrating on the Japanese offerings here, as the teppanyaki grill surrounded by granite counters is simply *the* place to be at in Kuala Lumpur.

In addition to teppanyaki, there's a comprehensive sushi and sashimi menu with fresh sashimi flown in daily from Japan. For the more adventurous, you can order *fubu* (puffer fish) seven days in advance, and there is a licenced *fubu* chef from Japan to cook it. Otherwise, choose from a tantalising array of Japanese dishes from Master grade *wagyu* teppanyaki, to noodles, tempura and more. Try our two recipes at home for a taste of what's on offer.

SHOOK! STARHILL GALLERY

Local timbers, polished and natural granite, and glass create a sensory, yet transparent, atmosphere within the open-plan restaurant. Conceptualized by Japanese designer, Yuhkichi Kawai, Shook! set new standards for hospitality design when it opened in 1999.

Butter Chicken Teppanyaki

The word "teppanyaki", derived from "teppan", which means "iron plate", and "yaki", the word for "grilled", "broiled" or "pan-fried", is a style of Japanese cuisine that uses an iron griddle to cook food. You can substitute with a thick-bottomed griddle or frying pan for similar results. The teriyaki sauce gives the chicken its sweet/sour flavour, while leeks add another dimension.

Serves 6
300 g chicken breast
salt and white pepper, to season
10 g tempura flour
10 g butter
30 ml teriyaki sauce
5 g leeks, thinly sliced and deep-fried
10 g mixed green salad

Method

Rub the salt and pepper onto the chicken, then coat the chicken with the tempura flour.

Fry the chicken with a little bit of vegetable oil.

Cut the chicken into smaller pieces, add a little bit of water and cook on a *teppan* or griddle pan for 5 minutes.

Lastly, add the teriyaki sauce and butter and continue to cook for another 5 minutes.

Serve on a plate, topped with deep-fried slices of leek, and a small mixed salad on the side.

Watari Karaage with Egg Yolk Tobiko

This is a light, fluffy, crispy fried crab starter that is accompanied with a tempura sauce. The crab should be cooked with its shell on, as this gives more flavour and a better colour after cooking.

Serves 6
300 g soft shell crab, cut into 18 pieces
5 ml *shoyu* sauce (Japanese soy)
20 g *tobiko* (flying fish roe)
20 ml egg yolk
30 g corn flour
5 g young ginger, grated
5 g white pepper
3 *ohba* leaves (Japanese basil)
5 g *togarashi* (Japanese chilli pepper)
1 lemon, cut into 6 wedges
360 ml Tempura Sauce (see below)

For the Tempura Sauce
500 ml full-flavored bonito stock
100 ml mirin
100 ml *yamasa shoyu*

Method

To make the tempura sauce, mix the three ingredients and boil up together. This will probably make a bit too much, but the sauce can be retained for another recipe.

Cut the soft shell crab into 18 pieces. Roll them in the *shoyu*, ginger and white pepper, then mix together with the corn flour and deep-fry in soy bean oil.

Once the crab turns light brown and crispy, drip the beaten egg yolk mixed with the *tobiko* onto the crab, and fry for a little longer until the crab becomes fluffy and crispy. Remove from fryer.

Cook the *ohba* leaves in the same manner (dipped in flour in the soy bean oil), for a few seconds. Remove from fryer.

Put the crab pieces onto a plate with the *ohba* leaves, top with *togarashi* and lemon wedges, and serve with tempura sauce on the side.

Sunday Brunch at Shook! Kuala Lumpur

On Sundays, visitors to Shook! can experience a themed brunch that combines fine food with champagne and various theatrics to keep everybody entertained. The photos here show a Shanghai theme; past months have seen Masquerades and more are planned for the future.

From noon until 6pm, the various areas of the restaurant are enlivened by an ensemble of stilt walkers, magicians, and a live band, along with an open kitchen providing pretty much any cuisine you can think of: Japanese, Mongolian barbeque, rotisserie, international salad bar, seafood, oyster bar, Chinese, Thai, Malay, a cheese platter, antipasti station and dessert bar. If that were not enough, there are lashings of champagne to wash it all down with.

Somehow, the space lends itself to the celebratory air that permeates throughout. Red lanterns and costumes, Chinese music, and plenty of entertainers mingle with guests in a setting more than a little suggestive of the Orient. For more information on Shanghai itself, turn overleaf.

OPPOSITE Signage is suitably exotic in red and gold; highly individual is the Shanghai belle embossed on a white chocolae cake.

BOTTOM Clockwise from top left: Goose noodles in large tureens; individual plating by a chef; costumed entertainer; sautéed *kai lan*; Shanghai braised duck; a phoenix lantern decoration.

AURORA

Shanghai Pearl of the Orient

OPPOSITE Two sides of Shanghai, separated by the Huangpu River: the modern region of Pudong (top) and the 1920s architecture of the Bund (below) could not be more different.

RIGHT AND BELOW Tea houses that closed during the Cultural Revolution are re-opening all over Shanghai — it's a relaxing sociable pastime to gossip over a cup of oolong, jasmine, *pu-erh*, *shui xian*, chrysanthemum flower or green tea.

It may be a cliché, but the area of old Shanghai snaking along the Bund really is redolent of the East. With its imposing 1920s architecture, deco decadence, dark woods and darker alleyways, it brings to mind stories of opium and opulence, intrigue and enterprise — and entertainment.

Between the wars, Shanghai's melting pot of East and West resulted in a town dedicated to the good life. Divided into three areas — the French Concession, the International Settlement and Greater Shanghai — the city attracted movers and shakers from across the globe. Foreign colonial powers may have theoretically called the shots, but there were Jews escaping from Nazi Germany, Russians fleeing the Russian Revolution, Chinese gangsters, and just about every other nationality jostling for a piece of the pie.

Cabaret shows, nightclubs, cocktail bars and high-end restaurants provided a heady backdrop to the city's mercantilism. Men in tuxedos, accompanied by *cheong-sam* clad sirens, danced the foxtrot, knocked back cocktails in highball glasses, did deals in shady dens and entertained lavishly. Much of the food served

So keen are the Shanghainese on late-night snacking, they even have a special phrase for after-midnight meals: "ye xiao". If that doesn't endear foodies to this city, nothing will!

was Western (as were the drinks), but locals and some of the more adventurous foreigners never neglected to try a *xiao chi* or one of the numerous "small eats" available on every street corner. The majority of these were home-prepared, with super fresh ingredients often cooked at lightning speed in a wok; they didn't rely on chillies or spices and tended to take their strong flavours from the ubiquitous soy, sugar, vinegar, garlic and ginger.

This tradition continues today, as the beast that is Shanghai has once again reawakened — and how! The modern city of Pudong across the river vies for views (and cash) with the Bund, while the city's 24 million inhabitants jostle and hustle compete and create for the future. They're as likely to grab a coffee and croissant as a cup of stinky tofu drenched in hot sauce or a plate of *xiao long bao* dumplings complete with straw to suck out the soup. Stylish, hard-working and competitive the city and its people are once again on the rise.

ABOVE, FROM LEFT TO RIGHT A street chef fills his dumplings, ready for steaming; cube's of Shanghai's famous freshly-cooked stinky tofu; even more famous *xiao long bao*, thin skinned dumplings filled with piping hot pork soup; grilled octopus; skewers of strawberries, dipped in sticky sugary sauce; grilled, crunchy birds-on-a-stick—cooked in front of your eyes.

RIGHT, ABOVE AND BELOW Despite the plethora of high rises, Shanghai is largely lived (and eaten) at street level. Most of the day and night-time cooking takes place on street corners and pavements.

OPPOSITE A sexy, semi-private booth is enclosed by sliding screens and carved wood latticework.

BELOW The Caviar Royal, the Time Bar's signature Kir Royale, is a molecular mixology creation from the head chef. Little pellets of fruit literally burst in your mouth as you take a sip of the Moet & Chandon vintage 2003 and "pearls" of crème de cassis combo.

Dining without Borders

The strapline for the Shook! restaurant brand is "dining without borders" and this is especially fitting in the international context of Shanghai. For, truly, this is an international city and has been for over 100 years (albeit with a brief 30-year hiatus in the Communist era). Situated in the heart of the Bund in The Swatch Art Peace Hotel, a newly renovated hotel in traditional art deco style, Shook! Shanghai is a sumptuous mix of old and new.

A stunning floor-to-ceiling wine cellar corridor is situated at the opening to the restaurant, which features very modern interiors with more than a touch of chinoiserie. There's an open kitchen, *shoji*-style screens and textural finishes in the form of lacquer, metallics and silk. It's a sexy space, with a variety of seating options, many with wonderful views over the river to the shimmering skyscrapers of Pudong beyond. Secluded private enclaves, elegant open dining and 12 seats in a granite-and-leather bar provide more than enough options for that special night out.

Like the KL Shook!, there is Malaysian cuisine, Thai, Chinese, Japanese and modern Western dishes. The focus is on interaction between guests, waiters and chefs — a theatrical culinary experience if ever there was one. The menu, for both liquid libations and food, is also "gender sensitive", with crafted dishes and drinks

LEFT TOP The brick veneer façade of The Swatch Art Peace Hotel, originally constructed in 1908 as the Palace hotel, on the site of the former Central hotel on busy Nanjing Road. Shook! is situated on the top floor and the roof terrace. The cupola on right (also seen opposite) offers a fabulous personalised dining option with views over the Bund and river to the modern high-rises of Pudong.

LEFT BELOW The hotel now contains 18 work-live apartments that are occupied by selected guest artists-in-residence from around the world, who enjoy a free six-month tenure. The dark Jacobean staircase houses one of the former residents' installations: a fabulous hanging 3-D sculpture of Chinese characters.

BELOW The busy open kitchen at Shook! with counter dining seats.

SHOOK! SHANGHAI

specifically for him and for her upon request. Overleaf, we share two signature dishes with you — a crispy egg noodle with seafood concoction and the famous snow white dancing prawns with hot mayonnaise and honey-glazed walnuts.

In keeping with the restaurant's philosophy of personalising dining experiences, there are also two private rooms to choose from (above and left). For larger gatherings, the Chiang-Soong Room is a sensual mix of wood panelling, gold leaf detailing and high ceilings. It has a historical pedigree that sets it apart: not only was the room the location of the first International Opium Conference in the early 1900s, it was also the venue of Chiang Kai Shek's engagement to Soong May Ling, his future wife. The other intimate dining option is a private corner cupola on the roof: here you really are dining beneath the stars.

In the summer months, the action moves upstairs to an al-fresco terrace where jazz-era music, cool breezes and river views provide more than enough in the way of entertainment. Who needs to recreate the Shanghai of old, when the Shook! roof terrace does it all for you?

Crispy Egg Noodles with Seafood Medley

This signature noodle dish at Shook! is an all round favourite. Yummy, chewy noodles — half wet from the sauce, half crispy — are flavoured with fresh-from-the-ocean seafood and local Asian vegetables for real comfort food credentials.

Serves 6

300 g egg noodles
6 medium-sized prawns, peeled, cleaned and heads removed
6 x 60 g fish fillets, cut into 2 to 3 cm slices
6 scallops, cleaned
18 sugar snaps
18 slices of carrots, medium-sized
1.8 litres chicken stock
6 tbsp oyster sauce
1 tbsp light soya sauce, to taste
12 g salt, to taste
8 g sugar, to taste
1 tbsp corn flour, to thicken the sauce
a few ginger slices and spring onions, sliced

Method

Steam the egg noodles for 5 minutes, then dip into boiling water for 1 minute before pan-frying for a minute or so in a little good quality cooking oil. Remove from pan, mould into an oval shape and place the noodles in the centre of a plate.

Steam the prawns, fish fillets and scallops for 5 minutes, then dip into boiling water for 1 minute before stir-frying for a couple of minutes, until cooked. Add the sugar snaps and sliced carrots and stir-fry for about 2 minutes until cooked. Lastly, add the chicken broth and seasoning including the corn flour; stir vigorously until all is combined and the sauce thickens.

Pour the sauce, with fish and veggies, over the noodles and garnish with slices of ginger and spring onions before serving.

Snow White Dancing Prawns with Hot Mayonnaise and Honey-glazed Walnuts

This "dancing prawn" dish has become eponymous with Shook! Shanghai. It looks elegant, tastes extraordinary, and immediately becomes a talking point at any table.

Serves 6
30 prawns, peeled, cleaned and heads removed
180 g lettuce
2 cups corn flour
120 g caramelised walnuts (see below)
12 leaves coriander, for garnish

For the Marinade
30 g corn flour
10 g salt
3 tbsp pure soy bean oil
1 g baking powder

For the Sauce
juice from 1/3 lemon
450 g mayonnaise
100 g sugar
100 g water

For the Caramelised Walnuts
350 g sugar
1 kg walnuts
1 tsp baking soda
sprinkling white sesame seeds, roasted

Method

To make the caramelised walnuts: Add the baking soda to a saucepan of water and boil together with the walnuts for 10 minutes. Rinse the walnuts through cold running water, then boil again for 1 to 2 minutes until cooked. Put the walnuts and sugar into a dry wok, then caramelise the sugar over a low heat until the walnuts are coated with the sugar evenly. Remove from heat, and set aside. When cool, heat some good quality cooking oil in a pan, deep fry the walnuts until golden brown and crunchy (approximately 3 to 5 minutes). Remove, sprinkle with white sesame seeds, set aside. When cool, chop into chunky pieces.

To make the sauce: Mix all the ingredients together until well combined.

Mix all the marinade ingredients, then soak the prawns in the marinade for 5 minutes. Remove and coat the prawns with the corn flour and deep fry in some good quality cooking oil until fragrant and crispy. Strain the excess oil, pat dry with paper towel, then coat the fried prawn with the sauce.

Slice the lettuce and put at the bottom of a flared glass. Place the prawns on top of the lettuce and sprinkle with chopped walnuts and coriander leaves, before serving.

Rare Vintages A Connoisseur's Dream

Many of the restaurants in this book have excellent wine cellars, a couple of them having some truly great ones. In addition to the high-end Bordeaux Burgundies and Côtes du Rhône from France, there are plenty of choices from the New World — from Australia and New Zealand, as well as north and south America Sommeliers are knowledgeable, and guests are advised wisely according to which cuisine they are choosing.

The two Shook! restaurants, however, have taken fine wine buying to a new level: Shook! in Kuala Lumpur's Feast Village is home to the entire Chateau Mouton-Rothschild Artisan Vertical Collection ranging from 1945 to 2005, while Shook! Shanghai is home to two other rare varietal Bordeaux — Chateau Cheval Blanc and Chateau d'Yquem, with vintages going back to 1945. As one of the sommeliers

notes: "An aged Bordeaux is hauntingly beautiful, blended into a harmonious composition of mature fruits, finely structured and very delineated." Those with a taste for claret are well looked after at both restaurants.

In addition, Shook! Shanghai has some exquisite cognacs, including the most expensive bottle of cognac ever sold, a 153-year-old unadorned bottle that fetched 1 million yuan and set a new world record. Its Hong Kong buyer is "storing" the bottle at the restaurant, with everybody wanting to know if she will ever actually drink it. Who knows?

CLOCKWISE FROM TOP LEFT
A glass of claret; at Shook! Shanghai — a bottle of St Emilion Bordeaux from 1968; an unmarked cognac with letter of authenticity; a beautiful Sauternes from Chateau d'Yquem, 1955; the wine cellar at the entrance to Shook! Shanghai; wine storage at Shook! in Feast Village, Kuala Lumpur.

Taste of Shanghai in Kuala Lumpur

Shanghainese cuisine differs from many of the main Chinese cuisines in that it isn't definitive unto itself; rather, it's comprised of dishes that are combined, refined, and amalgamated from cuisines that hail from various regions surrounding the city. As such, it borrows, it experiments, it begs — thereby producing dishes that become authentic in themselves.

Take the famous sweet and sour soup: Many people call this Shanghainese but in fact it originally came from Sichuan, and Shanghai chefs refined it into today's dish. The Shanghai dumpling (*siew loong pau*) is another example: Such dumplings are simply wonton wrapped *dim sum*, but the addition of the soy sauce and ginger accompaniment makes it more Shanghainese.

In fact, many Shanghainese dishes are characterised by the use of soy sauce, sugar, rice wine and rice vinegar, and are often cooked slowly. The tastes can be very strong, and the dishes dark in colour. Braised pigs trotters in brown sauce and Shainghai braised pork are two popular dishes, as is hairy crab.

SHANGHAI, JW MARRIOTT KUALA LUMPUR

ABOVE AND LEFT The circular dining room at JW Marriott's Shanghai is a sumptuous mix of gold, red and dark woods with delicate calligraphy and murals.

At Shanghai, the signature restaurant at Kuala Lumpur's JW Marriott, the chefs source such items as hairy crab from Shanghai itself, but also combine Shanghai produce with local ingredients. They aren't averse to using Western ingredients either, as evidenced by innovative fried noodles cooked with lobster and truffle oil. In fact, as long as they are improving on original Shanghainese cuisine and keeping to traditional flavours and cooking methods, they are all for experimentation.

An evening meal or lunch at this elegant, oriental-style restaurant is a real pleasure. Both round and square tables are set upon a deep red carpet, and walls are tastefully decorated with Chinese murals and motifs. There are also three private dining rooms, if you prefer. See overleaf for two of Shanghai's recipes.

Steamed Chicken in Chinese Rice Wine

Shao Xing wine is one of the most famous varieties of Chinese yellow wine fermented from rice. It originates from the region of Shaoxing, in the Zhejiang province adjacent to Shanghai and imparts an anise-like flavour to this juicy, tender chicken dish.

Serves 6

1 chicken, 1.5 kg in weight
15 g spring onions
10 g ginger
40 g dried scallops
280 ml Shao Xing rice wine
120 g salt
3 litres water
12 small stalks of Chinese vegetable, such as *kai lan* or similar

Method

Place the spring onions, ginger, dried scallops, 200 ml rice wine and salt into a saucepan filled with 3 litres of water. Bring to the boil, then add the whole chicken and simmer with the lid on for 30 minutes.

Remove the chicken, cut into six portions and place on plates.

Take 200 ml of the chicken broth, add another 80 ml of Chinese rice wine, and pour over the chicken. Sprinkle a little salt and sugar on top and serve with the vegetables on the side.

Deep-fried Mandarin Fish with Sweet and Sour Sauce

The so-called mandarin fish is a Chinese perch (Siniperca chuatsi), a freshwater fish that is yellow, green or brown in colour with many irregular black spots and patches. It can be substituted with grouper or marble golby, if unavailable.

Serves 6
850 g mandarin fish
25 g green beans, chopped
50 g tomatoes, chopped
50 g onions, finely diced
50 g sea cucumber, chopped
80 g prawns, sautéed
25 g pine nuts
1 kg potato flour
2 litres cooking oil

for the Marinade:
10 ml Shao Xing rice wine
5 g salt
100 g sugar
100 g tomato ketchup
15 g vinegar
5 g white pepper powder
splash ginger syrup, for seasoning and flavouring
splash egg gravy, to mix the seasoning and act as a thickener

Method

Wash the fish and slice at least half way into the fish's body in a criss-cross pattern. This allows the flavour of the sauce to penetrate the flesh, and also helps with presentation.

Mix the marinade ingredients together thoroughly, and marinade the fish. Then dip the fish in the potato flour and deep-fry until crispy.

In another wok, stir-fry the beans, tomatoes, onions and sea cucumber with 1 teaspoon rice wine at a high temperature for around 30 seconds.

Mix it all up and spoon over the fish on a large serving plate.

Lastly, sprinkle the pine nuts and cooked shrimps on top — and serve immediately.

"Anything that walks, swims, crawls, or flies is edible"

Old Cantonese Saying

Cantonese food is better known than Shanghainese cuisine outside of China, because so many people from the regions around Guangzhou (Canton) have emigrated to all corners of the globe. This vast diaspora of Cantonese has also diversified and adapted key dishes to take into account ingredients from the new areas in which they settled.

In its purest form, typical Cantonese cuisine strives to preserve the natural freshness and flavour of its ingredients. A Cantonese chef would consider it a culinary sin to produce a dish that was overcooked or too heavily seasoned. A major characteristic of Cantonese cuisine is that it uses very little in the way of spices. Instead, ginger, shallots, sugar, salt, soya sauce, rice wine, starch and oil are used. From time to time, five spice powder and pepper are also used in small qunatities. Preserved items such as pickled *bok choy* or raddish, salted and fermented tofu, dried shrimp, and salted fish are other popular flavourings.

LEFT A hawker-stall chef uses a cleaver to chop a side of pork belly.

OPPOSITE & BELOW Literally meaning "to touch your heart", dim sum consists of a variety of dumplings, steamed in bamboo baskets, and other goodies. It is inextricably linked to the Chinese tradition of *yum cha* or drinking tea. From opposite bottom, and left to right: *har gau* containing shrimp; *pau* or steamed bun for pork; *siew mai* containing pork; slices of pork; and egg tarts or *dan tat*, a custard pastry.

In addition to the staples of pork, beef and chicken, Cantonese cuisine includes almost all edible food such as snakes, snails, insects, worms, chicken's feet, duck's tongues, and entrails. Unlike other Chinese cuisines, the Cantonese usually serve soup in the form of a clear broth before a meal. Chinese herbal medicines are sometimes added to the clay pot, to make the soup nutritious and healthy.

Due to Guangzhou's proximity to the South China sea, cooking live seafood is a speciality. Prawns, shrimps, scallops, lobster and crab are in plentiful supply and many Chinese restaurants maintain live seafood tanks. The freshest seafood is odourless, and is best cooked by steaming with a little ginger and spring onions. Other prized Cantonese dishes include suckling pig, roasted barbeque pigeon, rice porridge and Cantonese dim sum.

LI YEN

ABOVE Poetically, the name Li Yen translates from the Cantonese as "beautiful garden".

OPPOSITE When we photographed Li Yen, the restaurant was sporting Chinese New Year decorations in the form of red tassels, swirling red fabric and strands of plum blossoms hanging from the ceiling. Nevertheless, at other times of the year, it looks equally atrractive.

With a long-time chef from Hong Kong and a host of hospitality awards under its belt, Li Yen at The Ritz-Carlton in Kuala Lumpur is a sure fire bet if fine Cantonese cuisine is your end game. Winner of the Five Star Diamond Award from the American Academy of Hospitality 12 years in a row, the restaurant specialises in authentic dishes from Guangdong province.

The chef is keen to point out that, in times past, Cantonese cuisine was generally considered the finest in China. It was the custom for Chinese emperors to travel the long distance down to the south, to Canton, purely to eat. In addition, many Cantonese chefs were summoned to Beijing's kitchens to bring new, tasty dishes for the delectation of the Imperial court. Today, the chef tries to do the same for his guests at Li Yen.

The restaurant sports an elegant Oriental interior with tasteful dark wooden screens, crisp tablecloths, and some old and new artistic flourishes. In addition to the main dining room, there are three private rooms for more intimate gatherings. The menu runs the gamut of Cantonese specialities, with yummy dim sum, plenty of double boiled soups, dishes sporting high-end ingredients such as abalone, as well as home-made tofu dishes, and plenty of noodle and veggie delights.

In general, Cantonese chefs tend to use a lot of double-boiled stock as it reduces and intensifies the flavour of dishes. Delicate foods, such as birds' nests and expensive herbal medicines, are placed in a covered ceramic jar and steamed for several hours. The technique ensures that there is no loss of liquid, essences or moisture — and vital nutrients are retained. Our double-boiled soup (overleaf) is tasty and health-giving, as the collagen from pigs' trotters strengthens joints and ligaments, while apples and apricots are full of antioxidants, flavinoids and vitamins.

Double-boiled Pig's Trotter and Apple Soup

Double steaming, sometimes also dubbed double boiling, is a Chinese cooking technique that allows no loss of liquid (or moisture) during the cooking process. This ensures that all the food's vital essences are retained, so it is a method often used for high-quality or expensive ingredients. It is said that this recipe has the benefit of strengthening the respiratory system.

Serves 6

- 500 g pig's trotters, seasoned with white pepper
- 500 g pork bone
- 4 kg water
- 5 red apples
- 2 pieces white fungus
- 10 g apricot
- 2 pieces candied apricot
- 10 g south apricot (*Prunus ameniaca*)
- salt, to season

Method

Boil the pig's trotters and bone in the water for 3 hours, making sure the pan has an airtight lid.

Add the apricot, candied apricot and south apricot for a further hour and 30 minutes. Then remove the pig's trotters together with the bones from the pan.

Add the salt, apples and white fungus and simmer for a further half hour. Remove the apples and trotters from the broth, chop them into small pieces and return them back into the broth.

Serve the broth in bowls.

Baked Spare Ribs with Chinese Tea Leaves

The marinade for this recipe renders the spare ribs slightly sticky, with a rich sweet taste that manages to be salty at the same time. Crispy tea leaves and shredded ginger give further flavouring — simply irresistible!

Serves 6

1.5 kg extra thick spare ribs, chopped into 4-inch-long rectangular shapes
240 ml soda water
6 tsps honey
3 tbsps maltose
1 tsp Maggi Seasoning Sauce
10 g ginger, shredded
10 g Chinese tea leaves, deep-fried

For the Marinade

1 tsp Maggi chicken powder
1 tsp baking soda
1 tsp yellow ginger powder
1 tsp peanut sauce
1 tsp mustard
salt, to taste
2 tsp sugar
2 tsp vinegar
1 tsp rock sugar
2 tsp Maggi Seasoning Sauce
2 tsp black soya sauce
½ tsp Bovril soup stock

Method

Soak ribs in the soda water (which is a slight meat tenderizer) for half an hour, then place under running water for 3 hours. Rinse, then pat dry.

For the marinade, in a large plastic bowl, mix all the ingredients together, then add the spare ribs and soak them in the container for 3 hours.

Bake each side of the spare ribs for 8 minutes in an oven set at 220°C.

Mix the honey, maltose and Maggi seasoning together, then heat up and pour over the spare ribs before arranging on a plate. Sprinkle the shredded ginger and deep-fried tea leaves on top — and serve immediately.

Lot 10, Kuala Lumpur

Every Malaysian has a childhood memory of a favorite dish they regularly sampled at their local hawker stall: be it *wanton mee*, Singapore noodles, the ubiquitous *dim sum*, or the unusual (to Western minds) so-called "carrot cake". It was this that led to the transformation of the basement of an old shopping mall in Kuala Lumpur into a new, buzzy and metropolitan food centre — but one that contains those old family memories captured through culinary culture and heritage.

Located on the corner of Jalan Bukit Bintang and Jalan Sultan Ismail, Lot 10 quickly became a huge success, even with the addition of some Western stalls and a couple of Korean ones. The imaginative layout recreates the cramped, narrow living quarters of centuries-old *hutongs* in Beijing; housing 32 restaurants and kiosks, it offers fare from some of KL's oldest hawker stores all set around a maze of colourful "alleyways".

Diners can sample all the perrenial favorites under one roof in an atmosphere that is more nostalgically Malaysian than Chinese. Dim sum trollies weave in and out of tables, the pusher calling out "*har gau, har gau*"; woks are fired up behind glass

Hawker centres sprung up in urban areas following rapid urbanisation in Asia in the 1950s and 1960s. They tended to attract family businesses, lured by the rents, a sense of community and access to clientele.

ABOVE AND OPPOSITE The décor at Lot 10 is full of fun signage, vintage advertisements and the type of furniture and fittings you find in old-fashioned local eateries. The slightly deco sign advertising Ho Weng Kee hangs down next to bare bulbs. This particular outlet has been serving up such delicacies as *wan ton mee* with *char siew*, beef brisket and pork ribs for three generations. Hon Kee Famous Porridge (top) has been making thick smooth wholesome porridge since 1949.

screens; there is the babble of market talk; a singular dedication to dining at simple clusters of tables and chairs; and the wonderful aromas of myriad family recipes.

The recipes overleaf come from the old family kitchen of Kong Tai (see chef on right). The original family hailed from Guangdong province in China, and the present-day chef is the grandson of Kong Tai's founder, who emigrated to Singapore decades ago. Exploring the food centres and hawker stalls of Singapore, experimenting with ingredients and improving the old family recipes led to the present-day chef being invited to cook at Singapore Day celebrations in New York City and London. He's now ensconsed happily at Lot 10 — and continues to cook what he now calls Singaporean food for locals and tourists alike.

LEFT The chef at Kong Tai cooks up a storm in his double wok kitchen; the recipes overleaf took him only minutes to produce, although the stock used is constantly bubbling away on another ring nearby.

BELOW, LEFT AND RIGHT During the Chinese New Year celebratory period, Lot 10 is decked out with red lanterns and other new year's decorations. The communal seating allows for conversations with strangers — but, more often than not, people are concentrating on the serious task of eating!

Tan Sri (Dr) Francis Yeoh, Managing Director of YTL Corporation, was the impetus behind Lot 10. A big fan of street food, he calls Lot 10 a "gourmet heritage food village" and bills it as the first food court of its kind in Malaysia.

Singapore Fried Prawn Mee

This is a Hokkien dish brought to southeast Asia by immigrants from Fujian province in China. There are different variants throughout the region, but the Singapore version uses both egg and rice noodles and gains its richness through the addition of pork lard and an aromatic prawn stock. This old family recipe from Kong Tai constitutes real food for the soul.

Serves 6

6 large farm eggs
210 g red chillies
35 g garlic, crushed
300 g bean sprouts
420 g soft vermicelli (rice noodles)
450 g yellow *mee* (egg noodles)
30 ml aromatic prawn stock (see opposite)
2 tbsp dried sole fish, chopped
15 ml pork lard
270 g lean pork, sliced into thin 4 cm long pieces
360 g prawns, de-shelled and cleaned
120 g chives, cut into 25 mm long pieces

Method

Crack open the eggs into a wok with the pork lard; add the garlic, red chilli and bean sprouts, and stir-fry for 2 minutes.

Add the vermicelli and yellow noodles, stir-fry together for another 2 minutes.

Finally, add a splash of prawn stock, fish pieces, pork slices and prawns. Heat until cooked through, then, before serving, add the chopped chives.

Serve in one large dish, or portion up into six separate bowls.

Raddish Cake

A popular hawker centre dish, the main ingredient is carrot cake, which confusingly is not like Western carrot cake and contains no carrot! Made from steamed rice flour, water and shredded white daikon, it is peppery and aromatic. When mixed with eggs, preserved raddish and other seasonings, it makes for a highly individual dish, much loved by cognoscenti.

Serves 6

30 g garlic, finely chopped
12 g shrimp paste
60 ml fish sauce
1.2 kg carrot cake (from an Asian market), fried
240 g chives, cut into 25 mm long pieces
60 g preserved raddish, finely chopped
360 g prawns, de-shelled and cleaned
6 large farm eggs
Chinese parsley, chopped, for garnish

for the Prawn Stock (makes 300 ml)

1 kg pork skin, cut into large pieces
2 kg pork bones
2 kg prawn heads
2 kg *lala* clams (can substitute with other clams, if unavailable)
5 kg lean pork, cut into big chunks
500 g rock sugar
120 g sole fish bones, dried
45 g salt
4–5 litres water

Method

To make the stock, boil all ingredients together for at least five hours. Strain and set aside.

Put a little cooking oil in a wok, and stir-fry the garlic, preserved raddish and prawns for about 30 seconds.

Add the fried carrot cake, shrimp paste, eggs and chives — and stir-fry for a further 2 minutes. Add a splash of the stock, and mix around a little longer.

Garnish with Chinese parsley before serving.

OPPOSITE Views out from Uncle Lim's restaurant to the tasteful, vernacular-style overwater guest rooms at Pangkor Island Resort.

BELOW The man himself! Humble and self-effacing, Uncle Lim has nevertheless cooked for countless guests during his 25 years at the helm of his highly successful restaurant at Pangkor Laut Resort.

A Culinary Institution *Uncle Lim's Kitchen*

Pangkor Laut Resort wouldn't be the same without Uncle Lim — both the restaurant and the man. Simply put, since its inception in the 1980s, the resort has always had an Uncle Lim's — and it would be inconceivable to imagine it any other way.

Perched on huge boulders, this open-air restaurant with a hospitable air looks out over the Straits of Malacca. Run by Uncle Lim, or Lim Fang Tat, for over 25 years, it pays homage to both its locale and local ingredients. There isn't a menu as such. Rather, Uncle Lim approaches guests, asks them what they like, then creates something personalised for them.

All Uncle Lim's recipes have been honed over the years through trial and error. The chef started in the F & B industry in his teens, and has developed his recipes ever since, constantly innovating, changing and improving to suit modern palates and to incorporate new and exciting ingredients. He likes simple food — with fresh ingredients and clean tastes — and is often inspired by the cooking of Hainan from where his parents originated.

Uncle Lim is also known for his Hock Chew dishes, many of which feature a sweet and sour sauce, and repeat guests rave about his Nyonya cooking where he doesn't hold back on his use of *belacan* (see overleaf). The chicken dish he shares with us (opposite) is a firm favourite: crunchy chicken pieces with more than a hint of calamansi and chewy sesame seeds — delicious.

Chinese Lime Chicken

Serves 6
1.2 kg boneless chicken legs
180 g corn flour
30 g sesame seeds
100 ml lime juice (preferably calamansi)
130 g plum sauce
120 g chilli sauce
600 ml cooking oil
salt and pepper, to taste

The combo of zesty, spicy/sweet/sour sauce and tender chicken gives this dish a super outdoorsy, summer feel. An added bonus is that it is pretty simple to make – and quick too.

Method

Slice the chicken legs and coat with corn flour and sesame seeds, then deep fry until they are golden in colour and crispy in texture (approximately 4 minutes).

Heat the oil in a wok, pour in the lime juice, plum and chilli sauces, then add the crispy chicken. Toss together in the pan for about 20 seconds.

Season to taste, then serve with hot, steamed jasmine rice.

Peranakan Cuisine A Heritage to Honour

Although the Chinese may have been trading in the Malay archipelago from as early as the 1st century, it is unlikely that they actually began to settle there until the 16th at the earliest. Certainly, from the 17th century onwards, there was a thriving community of Chinese in Malacca (and other Straits Settlement ports) — and the assimilation of such with the local Malay community resulted in a new generation of Chinese-Malays: the Peranakan, or Straits Chinese.

Over the next couple of centuries, this community gained in wealth, prominence and stature, all the while developing and nurturing a distinct cultural heritage that has survived to date. They faithfully maintained Chinese traditions, yet also incorporated elements from the local culture — their language, dress and architecture were a delightful mix of Malay and Hokkien, and — most importantly (for our purposes!) — they amalgamated their two culinary styles.

As in all areas of Peranakan life, the art of cooking was an expressive medley of eclecticism. We see the Malay fondness for chillies, *belacan* (dried shrimp paste), and coconut milk incorporated into traditional Chinese dishes; Hokkien cakes and

OPPOSITE A local eatery along Jonker street serves up sardines and veggies for the lunchtime crowd.

BELOW, LEFT TO RIGHT Market fare includes *kesumba* flowers and *buah keluak*, nuts used frequently in Peranakan cuisine; a plate of rice and ladies' fingers with other veggies; sliced red and green chillies; and crackers that need to be fried before they can be eaten.

dumplings were liberally scented with tropical pandan leaves; and local Malay dishes were modified to suit the Chinese palate. Such was the assimilation that, by the early 20th century, offerings to the ancestors would have been as likely to include spicy coconut curry as Hokkien *mee*.

In a Peranakan household, the kitchen was known as the *perut rumah* or "stomach of the house" — and much of social and religious life was expressed through food. Kitchen skills were passed down through generations of Nyonya women (the women were called Nyonya, the men Baba) and every well-brought-up Nyonya would have been expected to have mastered many dishes.

Today, Peranakan cuisine is little known internationally, but in Malaysia, Singapore and Indonesia it is justly celebrated locally — with everybody having their own favourite dish. Pungent, spicy and fragrant, Nyonya cooks say it is all in the preparation — which can literally take hours. Extended periods of marination, all spices pounded fresh, only the freshest of ingredients and the best cuts — all contribute to this delightfully distinctive cuisine.

The 600-year-old port of Malacca is a charming place to sample authentic Nyonya cuisine. Spend some time wandering through the old quarter, where picturesque Chinese shophouses line narrow streets adjacent to the historic river, and see all manner of preparing, cooking and eating. Then turn into 188 Jalan Bunga Raya to the sanctuary of The Majestic Malacca, an authentically restored Peranakan mansion turned heritage hotel, and relax for a culinary feast.

Hotel chefs have shared a couple of savouries with us — Chicken Cincaluk and Udang Kuah Nenas — and also given us plenty of information about Peranakan cooking. They point out that in addition to the very particular flavour of *belacan*, Nyonya dishes use galangal, turmeric and lemongrass, as well as chilli and aromatic leaves such as curry, pandan and Kaffir lime. These Malay flavours permeate throughout, but you'll also find some imported English provisions in the kitchen: As dedicated Anglophiles, the Peranakans were keen on products such as Bovril, Milkmaid condensed milk and Lea & Perrin's Worcester sauce!

ABOVE The Bar at The Majestic Malacca is a mix of clubby colonial and Straits Chinese, with dark wood and classic Peranakan floor tiles. It serves up a range of whiskies, cocktails and other drinks.

OPPOSITE On either side of the blackboard are two desserts from The Majestic kitchen: Sour Plum Shake and Nyonya Cendol, the latter being a classic made from coconut milk, rice flour pieces, shaved ice and palm sugar.

Chefs at The Majestic encourage you to learn more at a cooking class hostec by the Peranakan Master Chef: not only will you take home some heritage recipes you'll delve into the history of each exquisite dish and expand your knowledge of aromatic ingredients. Then it will be time to sit down in the formal Mansior restaurant, or put your feet up in The Bar. As with the rest of the hotel, these spaces have been decorated in authentic Peranakan style with the pastel colours so beloved by the Straits Chinese, hand-crafted swing doors or *pintu pagar*, tiles imported from China and typical marble tables and bentwood chairs.

There's nothing like heritage dining in authentic, comfortable surrounds. And fo those with a sweet tooth, there's always the eponymous Sago Gula Melaka — a dessert that tastes a bit like crème caramel, yet has hints of coconut and palm sugar as well (see page 130).

THE MAJESTIC MALACCA

The Majestic began life in the 1920s as a mansion to house the family of Guangzhou-born businessman Leong Long Man. Unfortunately in 1931 he died and, as the family fortunes dwindled, the family were forced to sell in the 1950s. The building became a guesthouse, then fell into disrepair, before being restored and re-opened by YTL as a beautiful boutique heritage hotel.

Udang Kuah Nenas

Combining Chinese culinary practices with local Malay ingredients is the basis of Nyonya cuisine, and this pineapple prawn curry is no exception. The honey pineapples grown around Malacca infuse sweetness into the broth, while the herbs and spices add a certain sourness. The result is a dish that is easy and light on the palate – but also rich, sharp and spicy.

Serves 6
600 g white prawns, cleaned and peeled
200 g pineapple, cubed
30 g shrimp paste
40 g lemongrass
250 ml coconut milk
200 ml water
½ tsp salt
1 tsp sugar
150 ml cooking oil

For the paste
150 g shallots, peeled
50 g garlic, peeled
40 g turmeric, crushed
20 g ginger, bruised
15 g galangal, bruised
20 g candlenuts
50 g red chilli

Method

Cut the pineapple into cubes, set aside.

Blend the paste ingredients, until a fine, smooth consistency is achieved. Set aside.

Spread the shrimp paste on a flat tray then toast in a salamander, or grill, for a few minutes.

Heat the oil in a wok and sauté the blended fine paste, the shrimp paste and the lemongrass together until the mix becomes a bit drier and more fragrant. Transfer to a saucepan, add water and the pineapple cubes, and stir; allow to simmer for about 15 minutes until the sweetness of the pineapple is released into the gravy.

Pour in the coconut milk and simmer for a further 2 to 3 minutes.

Add the prawns and simmer over a low heat for a further 10 minutes or so until they are cooked through.

Add sugar and salt to taste before serving.

Chicken Cincaluk

Cincaluk, a fermented shrimp condiment from Malacca and Penang, is easily obtainable today in Asian food stores. The main ingredient is geragau — tiny little shrimps found off the west coast of Malaysia. Fermented with salt water and sugar, cincaluk can be an acquired taste: its pungent flavour and aroma permeates this typical Nyonya chicken dish.

Serves 6
650 g chicken legs with skin, cut into large pieces
180 g plain rice, cooked

For the spicy paste
150 g shallots, sliced
50 g garlic, chopped
40 g fresh turmeric, chopped
20 g candlenuts, crushed
20 g ginger, chopped
2 Kaffir lime leaves, julienned
40 g lemongrass, finely sliced
30 g red chilli, finely sliced
70 g onion, finely sliced

For seasoning
100 g *cincaluk* (preserved shrimp sauce), strained
200 ml full-bodied chicken stock
8 g sugar

Method

Finely blend paste ingredients together and sauté in a hot pan with vegetable oil for 3 minutes or until fragrant.

Add the chicken pieces and continue to cook for another 4 minutes without covering. Then, pour in the stock, strained *cincaluk* and sugar for seasoning, cover and bring to the boil. Simmer for about 6 minutes, until the chicken pieces are fully cooked.

Serve immediately with plain rice.

Sago Gula Melaka

Gula Melaka or palm sugar has a richer flavour and darker colour than Indian jaggery, and is made from the sap of the coconut tree flower bud. After it is collected and boiled, it is poured into bamboo tubes, three to five inches long, until it sets. Both it, and the coconut milk, give this quintessential Malacca dessert its flavour — as the sago itself is tasteless

Serves 6
200 g sago
400 ml coconut milk
300 g palm sugar (*gula* Melaka)
250 ml water
2 pandan leaves
10 g salt, to taste

Method

Bring a large pan of water to the boil, then pour in the sago. Stir constantly, so no lumps appear. When the sago looks crystal clear and has floated to the surface, it is cooked (this should take approximately 10 minutes). Strain and rinse with cold water a couple of times to remove any remaining starch.

Add the salt to the coconut milk; set aside.

Spoon the sago into jelly moulds, and chill until set (about 1 hour).

While waiting for the sago, heat the *gula* Melaka and water, along with the pandan leaves, in a saucepan over a low heat until the sugar dissolves.

To serve, turn the sago moulds out on to a plate or bowl, top with a little coconut milk and *gula* Melaka, and present at the table.

Serves 6
500 g glutinous flour
200 g sweet potato
100 ml water
200 g palm sugar (*gula* Melaka)
250 g coconut flesh, freshly grated
20 g salt

Ondeh-ondeh

The word ondeh-ondeh refers to any sweet that is in the shape of round balls, so this recipe should be called ondeh-ondeh keledek, the latter being the Malaysian word for sweet potato. Often, this doughy snack is green in colour as it is flavoured with pandan leaf or essence of pandan. Ours are delightfully orange though, taking their colour from the local sweet potatoes.

Method

Break up the palm sugar into small pieces; set aside.

Peel, cook and mash the sweet potatoes; set aside.

Sieve the glutinous flour into a large bowl, add the mashed sweet potatoes and water, and mix well. When combined, knead into a dough, then fashion into small balls roughly 2.5 cm in diameter. Make a hole in the centre of each ball and fill with small pieces of palm sugar, then re-roll again to hide the filling.

Bring a saucepan of water to the boil and add the dough balls. When they float to the surface of the water, remove and place on a draining tray.

Add salt to the freshly grated coconut, then roll the cooked glutinous balls in the coconut — and serve.

Nyonya Kuih Tea Time at The Majestic Malacca

In recent years, the headlong rush towards modernity in Malacca has resulted in some improvements in living standards, but it has also meant that many traditions are being lost. As such, it is all the more important to preserve the culinary traditions of the Straits Chinese.

One of the areas beloved by all Peranakan foodies is the Nyonya *kuih*. Bite-sized snacks, cakes, or desserts, *kuih-muih* include cakes, cookies, dumplings, puddings and pastries, and are usually made from rice or glutinous rice and are most often steamed, not baked. They come in a variety of rainbow colours and flavours, with Malacca favoring the *gula* Melaka (palm sugar) ingredient and the bright blue dye of the blue pea flower or *bunga telang*.

Many Nyonya *kuih-muih* are simply adaptations of Malay snacks or Malay versions of sweet cakes and desserts, but many others are based on family recipes. Traditionally, *kuih-muih* making was the domain of elderly grandmothers and aunties, for whom the only method for cooking was by *agak agak* (approximation). Therefore, every family had its own take on a particular *kuih*: weighing scales were often set aside and mixes measured on feel, consistency and touch rather than kilos and grams.

At The Majestic Malacca, afternoon tea in The Library at The Mansion with a selection of *kuih-muih* is a delight. There's a wonderful local spin with typical delicacies like *pai tee*, shredded vegetable "baskets" with shrimp paste, and Nyonya *chung*, sticky rice dumplings wrapped in pandan leaf and filled with shredded coconut.

ABOVE Serving tea and *kuih* in The Library at The Majestic Malacca is a waitress in typical Nyonya dress: a sarong and *kebaya* or traditional blouse in Peranakan pastel shades.

Bali's Bounty

Bali has to be one of the most extraordinary places on the planet: variously called The Island of the Gods, The Morning of the World, The Last Paradise, out of the main tourist areas at least, it is still untouched, pristine and pure. There is the lushness of mountain and rice terrace territory, the beauty of volcanic sand beaches, the intricacy and delicacy of age-old temple architecture. Most importantly, there is the innate goodness of the population: a heritage-rich, spiritual people straddling past and future with admirable aplomb.

Unsurprisingly, food is central to Balinese culture. The Balinese say that there is no meal without rice, so everywhere you look, you'll see the cultivation of paddy rice. Water is one of the few items that isn't abundant in Bali, so every farmer plants, harvests and irrigates according to a network of water-sharing associations called *subak* that were devised over 1,000 years ago. Everybody respects this

RIGHT AND OPPOSITE Naturally, the market is where people head for the daily shop. Fruit, vegetables, spices and pulses are all readily available in most towns. Fish are best bought on the beach in the early morning when the catch is brought in.

OPPOSITE TOP Some women spend their lives making offerings for the gods. Set on a tray of woven young coconut leaves, small foodstuffs, flowers and other paraphernalia are presented to the gods daily.

system; everybody contributes to its maintenance; and everybody pays homage to Dewi Sri, the highly venerated Goddess of Rice, at various times during the rice cycle.

In addition to rice, there is ordinary everyday food and there is ceremonial food. The former is simple — vegetables, a little bit of meat or fish, and rice — and it is either eaten at home or in the local *warung*. This is the place for a snack and a gossip, and offers more variety than the family kitchen: Chinese mariners left their mark in the *bakso* Chinese meatball soup seller and Chinese–style steamed buns with sweet or savory fillings called *bakpao* are a perrenial favourite. Non-Chinese influenced dishes make use of native fruits — mangosteens, rambutans, jackfruits — with bananas and jackfruit often sliced and fried into *krupuk*, or crispy chip snacks.

Most Hindu ceremonies include an edible component, with pork and duck usually finding their way into festival menus. *Babi guling* is a spit-roasted pig stuffed with chillies, turmeric, garlic and ginger, while *bebek betutu* is roast duck wrapped in banana leaf — both are full of flavour and come highly recommended.

Fresh Spa Cuisine *in Tembok*

In order to experience the "real" Bali, it is necessary to get away from the main tourist centres and seek a location where life is governed by authentic Balinese principles — balance, harmony, spirituality. One such place is Spa Village Resort Tembok, Bali, a destination spa on the island's secluded north-east coast. Set directly on the beach, with the majestic Gunung Agung volcano and rice terraces as a backdrop, it is the ideal place in which to immerse oneself in the genuine, untouched spirit of Bali.

The resort offers a number of personal wellness programmes that honour the deep-seated culture of the island, as well as a stress-free environment where coconut palms and manicured lawns mingle with simple wood, thatch and local stone

architecture, the sea and horizon. Most of the staff is from the local village of Tembok and the tailored rituals, programmes and experiences are extremely authentic.

Naturally, the cuisine follows this cue: The core philosophy of the kitchen is fresh, natural and organic — enhancing the spa experience. The area's black volcanic soil is perfect for growing veggies, so there is a also a sustainable, eco-ethos going on with the local farming community. Each morning, the chef inspects the catch of the day 50 metres down the beach and brings back a selection of what is on offer, most likely red snapper, mackerel, mahi mahi, tuna or barracuda. He also buys greens from Kintamani, less than an hour's drive away, then plans a hand-crafted menu for the day. Every day is different depending on what he can source to hand.

ABOVE The cool, inviting pool, situated between garden and beach, is the magnet of the resort. The large open-air pavilion behind serves as the restaurant.

OPPOSITE Small details — flower arrangements and handmade items — contribute to the folksy appeal.

Honouring Balinese healing traditions is the resort's raison d'etre, but it is not only the spa that provides this service: it also comes in the form of wholesome food, nutritious snacks, tropical juices, ancient jamu and more.

OPPOSITE TOP The resort's accommodations combine Balinese elements with luxurious comfort.

ABOVE, LEFT AND OPPOSITE, FAR LEFT Nutritious meals, snacks and juices are served in the open-sided Wantilan which boasts sea views from a breezy outdoor terrace.

OPPOSITE, MIDDLE The pool with attendant *balés* is perfect for lounging, basking and slowing the rhythm of daily life.

The resort's little restaurant, aptly named Wantilan after the open-sided pavilion found in every Balinese community, is a hybrid of the traditional and the tropical with an emphasis on healthy, fresh flavours. Breakfast includes freshly brewed coffee that is organically grown on the slopes of Kintamani, local fruits, granolas and yoghurt, then lunch and dinner present a variety of fresh-from-the-sea and -field dishes cooked from the soul. As with home cooking, food is wholesome, uncomplicated and energy-giving. We are happy to share two recipres from Spa Village Resort Tembok, Bali overleaf.

Kare Ayam

This typical Balinese chicken curry is imbued with the flavours of southeast Asia — ginger, turmeric, chilli and the ever-present rich creamy coconut milk, the trees of which are to be found all over the island. Spicy and pungent, the dish is best served with steamed rice.

Serves 6
400 g free range chicken, cut into pieces
360 ml chicken stock
200 ml coconut milk
160 g eggplant, cut into strips
160 g cauliflower, cut into florets
100 g courgettes, cut into oblongs
100 g long beans, cut into smaller pieces
1 tsp salt and pepper

For the Paste
100 g galangal, chopped
150 g shallots, chopped
100 g garlic, chopped
50 g turmeric, crushed
100 g red chilli, chopped
80 g candlenuts, chopped
100 g Chinese ginger, chopped
50 g shrimp paste
splash cooking oil

Method

Grind all the paste ingredients (except shrimp paste and cooking oil) together and sauté with the shrimp paste and a little bit of oil.

Add the chicken pieces and sauté in the paste for 3 to 5 minutes, then add the chicken stock. Allow to simmer for 10 minutes. Add the vegetables and, lastly, pour in the coconut milk.

Continue to simmer until the aroma of the coconut has come out, then add salt and pepper to taste before serving, preferably with steamed rice.

Serves 6

- 600 g fish, minced (baracuda or swordfish are recommended)
- 1 tbsp shallots, chopped and fried
- 1 tbsp garlic, chopped and fried
- $^{1}/_{3}$ cup coconut milk, thick
- 3 tbsp basic spice paste (see below)
- 4 bird's eye chillies, sliced
- 1 tsp salt
- 1 tsp black peppercorns, crushed
- 12 pieces banana leaf, cut in 20 cm (8 inch) squares
- 12 *salam* leaves (Indonesian bay leaves)

for the Basic Spice Paste

- 10 g turmeric, crushed
- 100 g shallots, sliced
- 50 g garlic, sliced
- 20 g galangal, sliced
- 20 g candlenuts, crushed
- 10 g Chinese ginger, sliced

Tum Ikan

Tum, leaf-wrapped bundles of highly seasoned food, are made with almost any ingredient in Bali, ranging from minced eels, to chicken, pork, beef or duck. Usually the ubiquitous banana leaf is employed for this purpose, as it adds a distinctive flavour and is easily sourced all over the island.

Method

For the spice paste, grind all the ingredients until smooth, then sauté for 3 to 5 minutes. Set aside.

Combine all the ingredients, except for the banana leaf pieces and *salam* leaves, and mix well. Fold a heaped tablespoon of the mixture into the centre of a banana leaf and wrap. Repeat for all 12 pieces. Steam parcels for about 15 minutes, until well cooked.

Scatter the *salam* leaves over the parcels, and serve with steamed rice.

RIGHT Spa Village Resort Tembok's *jamu* lady visits the resort twice a day, carrying her *jamu* on her head.

BELOW Illustrating the fact that *jamu* is primarily a cottage industry, banana leaf stoppers are used as corks. Ingredients, such as these turmeric rhizomes, are grown locally.

An Ancient Tradition *Jamu*

The Indonesian practice of making and drinking *jamu*, a type of herbal health drink, goes back thousands of years. Once integral in every family, with mothers passing recipes down to daughters, it has declined considerably as the archipelago has modernised. However, with the growth in the spa industry, *jamu* has begun to re-emerge.

At Spa Village Resort Tembok, Bali, a local villager comes by twice a day carrying (as is traditional in Bali) her homemade *jamu* bottles in a basket on her head. Made from plants, roots, barks, leaves, honey, fruits and more, her *jamu* is more than a mere tonic. It is a revitaliser, a strengthener, a beauty aid and a health-giver.

Traditionally, Indonesians have subscribed to a philosophy that inner health and outer beauty are one and the same. A healthy body breeds a healthy mind; a spiritually secure person has emotional stability. Moderation in daily life and sensible lifestyle practices help such an outcome. So does a daily glass of *jamu*.

Even though *jamu* varies wildly from village to village, most recipes contain turmeric for its astringent qualities, tamarind for blood cleansing and ginger for flavouring and aiding digestion. Honey is often added to mask the bitter taste. We offer you a couple of options — Jamu Kunyit Asam for women, Jamu Beras Kencur for men — to give you an exotic alternative to the smoothie or health drink.

Jamu Kunyit Asam

Tamarind & Turmeric Tonic

Method

Remove the skin from the turmeric, and wash it under running water. Finely slice.

Bring a saucepan with 1.5 litres of water to the boil, then add the slices of turmeric, the tamarind paste, the palm sugar and salt.

Boil for 10 minutes, set aside. Allow to cool, transfer to an airtight bottle and store in the refrigerator.

Before serving (either warm or chilled), run the liquid through a sieve, so the root debris is retained.

Makes 6 glasses
'50 g turmeric root
'50 g tamarind paste
100 g palm sugar
pinch salt
1.5 litres water

Jamu Beras Kencur

Rice & Finger Root Tonic

Method

eel the finger root (a type of hinese ginger) and wash it nder running water. Then mash : to extract the juice.

ring a saucepan with 1.5 litres f water to the boil, then add the amarind paste, cinnamon sticks, loves and palm sugar. Boil for 0 minutes, then set aside, and llow to cool.

Add the finger root juice and rice flour, plus a pinch of salt, and mix thoroughly. Transfer to an airtight bottle and store in the refrigerator.

Before serving (either warm or chilled), run the liquid through a sieve, so the root debris/cinnamon sticks etc are retained.

Makes 6 glasses
00 g rice flour
50 g tamarind paste
50 g finger root
00 g palm sugar
50 g cinnamon sticks
10 cloves
pinch salt
1.5 litres water

Thai Theatrics

Harmony in a Bowl

Ideally, a Thai meal should be a harmonious blend of spicy, sweet, sou and salty — and oftentimes the spicy element leads the way! Usually, a number o dishes are served together with rice and condiments, and meals are a sociable affair

Everybody has their favourite dish: the hot, sour and fragrant *tom yam goong* o spicy prawn soup with lemongrass; *som tam* or green papaya salad; the rice flou vermicelli *phad Thai*, redolent with peanuts, beansprouts and pickled white raddish or one of the many green, yellow or red curries. Bursting with different flavours and textures, they are united in their use of fresh produce and complex seasoning

There tends to be quite a difference in both produce and taste of dishes depending on the region from where they originated. In the north and north east Lao and Burmese influences can be seen, and many northern dishes are Chinese ir origin. Wok cooking and the technique of stir-frying are both Chinese introductions as is *chok* or rice porridge and *khao kha mu* (stewed pork with rice). In the south

OPPOSITE In the royal court in past times, traditional dance often accompanied feasts or banquets.

ABOVE Clockwise from top left: *phad Thai* with prawns; Thai holy basil; crab claw in batter; ubiquitous condiments in a Thai food hall; takeaway mango, coconut milk and sticky rice in banana leaf; spicy, sweet and sour Thai salad.

Thai curries tend to contain coconut milk and turmeric; in the north, lime juice is a popular ingredient in many dishes and soups.

Nevertheless, there is a unique "Thai identity" to the country's cuisine: the flavours are aromatic, hot and sour and herbs such as lemongrass, galangal and kaffir lime leaves are widely used, along with fried basil leaves and the ubiquitous *nam pla* or Thai fish sauce. Preparation can be long and complicated, but the results speak for themselves. Also, unlike other Asian cuisines, Thai aesthetics shine in Thai food: artistic presentation is one of the cuisine's hallmarks.

Teeq Brasserie Restaurant in the Sky

LEFT The interior of Teeq is a sleek mix of textures and tones. The undulating ceiling is without doubt its most arresting feature.

ABOVE RIGHT The outdoor deck in the evening is blowy and breezy; subtle floor-level lighting helps with both atmosphere and visibility.

BELOW Signage—as at all YTL outlets—is imaginative and modern.

Downtown Kuala Lumpur is the last place you'd expect to find a forest, but sure enough, on the roof of one of the city's high-rises there's a veritable Forest in the Cityscape — replete with grass, miniature hedges, wooden pathways, and plenty of trees. A respite from the city, it also houses a brasserie that surprises at every turn.

Seating choices are at an al-fresco seating cluster between the lawn and a modernist stainless steel bar or within the large oblong glass-encased restaurant itself. Inside, an undulating ceiling made from long wooden slats brings a bit of the outdoor in, while floor-to-ceiling glass windows are sheathed in planters of bamboo. The best spot, however, is the outdoor deck where city views vie for attention with fully-grown trees, a hedge of cascading purple thunbergia, and a beautifully manicured lawn.

The food, a mix of international and Asian, comes from a menu that is designed to reflect the city's cosmopolitan nature. There are some unusual dishes, but plenty of well-loved favourites: think burgers with shoe-string fries, spicy chicken wings, a selection of noodle and fried rice dishes, as well as soups and salads.

The two Thai dishes we feature here are staples on any Thai menu worth its salt, combining as they do the sweet with the sour, the spicy with the lemony. Bringing to mind carefree beach days under swaying palms, they are summery and light, not to mention quick and easy to prepare and cook. What could be more beguiling than a Thai-style feast beneath the stars — but firmly set in the city?

Larb Gai

This chicken salad is not cooked with oil so it has a light, summery feel. It can be served simply with lettuce or other green vegetables, and is spicy, herby and healthy.

Method

Mince the chicken with some salt and the finely chopped garlic.

Heat the stock, add the minced chicken and simmer until the chicken is cooked through.

Strain the cooked minced chicken out from the chicken stock and place it in a bowl.

Season the minced chicken with lime juice and fish sauce, stir well. Add the shallots, bird's eye chillies, mint and spring onions into the mixture.

Lastly sprinkle with ground roasted rice, and garnish with coriander leaves.

Serve with cabbage, snake beans and cucumber, or any green lettuce that you prefer.

Serves 6

300 g skinless chicken breast
5 g small garlic cloves, finely chopped
500 ml chicken stock
10 ml lime juice
5 g bird's eye chillies, chopped
10 ml fish sauce
5 g red shallots, sliced
3 g mint leaves, shredded
3 g spring onions, chopped
5 g roasted rice, ground
3 g coriander leaves, for garnish

Pla Tod Grob

This crispy deep-fried fish dish is accompanied by a typically Thai-style sweet-sour marinade. Because the fish is only cooked for about six minutes, it retains its moisture, especially when doused in the wonderfully piquant sauce. It is perfect with plain rice and/or a raw papaya salad.

Method

Season the fish with salt, then deep fry for about 6 minutes or until it turns golden brown. Set aside.

Mix all ingredients (except fish and garnish) together in a bowl. Make sure the taste is sweet and sour.

Place the deep fried fish on to a serving plate and pour all the well-mixed sauce on top.

Garnish with coriander and serve with steamed rice.

Serves 6

1 whole sea bass (approximately 1.2 kg)
18 g flaked sea salt, to marinate the fish
1.2 litres peanut oil for deep frying

For the Thai-style Sauce

15 g lemongrass, chopped
15 g spring onions, chopped
15 g red chilli, chopped
10 ml fish sauce
10 g sugar
15 ml lime juice
100 g roasted peanuts, ground into a coarse texture
10 g shallots, chopped
450 g chicken stock
10 g young ginger, chopped
10 g mint, shredded
3 g coriander leaves, for garnish

Sabai Sabai

Beach Life, Thai-style

Literally, *sabai* translates as "well", and the expression *sabai sabai* is used in Thailand to show that everything is relaxed, everybody is fine, and the world is as it should be. This perfectly encapsulates the feeling at The Surin, a recently revamped resort nestled amongst coconut palms on sublime Pansea beach.

Named after the Sanskrit *Sura* which means God and *In-tar* or *Indra*, the Hindu Lord of Heaven, the Surin is — simply put — heavenly. Such lofty nomenclature is not misplaced, as the Ed Tuttle design mixes sybaritic luxury with a laid-back vibe, and both service and accommodations are of the highest quality.

Naturally, there are plenty of eating options: fresh seafood barbecues on the beach, spicy hot and sour soups and red and green curries in both main and beach restaurant, and plenty of snacks poolside. Accompanied by genuinely friendly service, every meal is a new experience. Try The Surin's recipes overleaf.

LEFT Tables are laid out along the white sand Pansea beach for a beach barbecue at The Surin.

RIGHT One of the many al-fresco dining spots at The Surin: overlooking the sea from some height, this deck has excellent sunset views.

TOP A little information booklet at the resort gives descriptions of the fruit you're likely to find in your room, and some of the exotic flowers used as decorations in the restaurants.

Haw Mok Talay

Not a terrine in the classical sense, but a custard-like steamed curry, haw mok talay has a velvety smooth taste and, surprisingly for a Thai dish, a lack of spiciness — so it is suitable for children. Traditionally made with fish and steamed in little cups made of banana leaf, the terrine is best served with steamed jasmine or organic brown rice.

Serves 6

180 g red snapper fillets, sliced as thinly as possible, then chopped finely
60 g squid, sliced into thin strips
60 g prawns, chopped finely
30 g *kreung gaeng kathi* (see below)
240 ml coconut milk (preferably fresh)
30 ml Thai fish sauce (*nam pla*)
12 g sugar
1 pinch turmeric powder
6 Kaffir lime leaves, julienned
30 g basil leaves
12 g red chillies, thinly sliced, for garnish
handful coriander leaves, for garnish

For the Kreung Gaeng Kathi
(Kathi Curry Paste)
200 g dry chillies, seeded and soaked
6 g salt
60 g galangal, peeled
60 g lemongrass
18 g Kaffir lime zest
6 g coriander root
90 g garlic
150 g shallots
18 g shrimp paste (optional)

Method

To make the curry paste, grind all the ingredients in a pestle and mortar until a smooth paste is achieved.

In a heat-proof bowl, mix 30 g of the curry paste with the coconut milk and turmeric powder until well combined; add the sliced fish and stir.

Add the prawns, squid, fish sauce and sugar, and mix thoroughly.

Add the lime and basil leaves, then place the bowl over a saucepan of simmering water and steam for about 8 to 10 minutes until a firm mousse is achieved.

Garnish with sliced chilli and coriander leaves and serve with rice.

Tom Kha Poo

This mildly spicy hot and sweet soup is known for the unique flavour of galangal, an ingredient often found in Thai cuisine. Though it is related to and looks like ginger, it has a citrusy, piney, earthy aroma that gives this soup its unusual taste. Embellished with the delicate flavour of fresh crab, lemongrass, lime leaves and coconut milk, tom kha poo is one of the Surin's tastiest soups.

Serves 6

1 ½ cups crab meat from blue crabs, poached
3 tbsp galangal, julienned
1 tsp turmeric powder or 2 slices fresh turmeric
2 tbsp lime juice, to taste
2 tbsp Thai fish sauce (*nam pla*)
3 cups coconut milk
4 shallots, sliced
5 bird's eye chillies (*prik khee nu*)
1 ½ tbsp lemongrass, chopped (white part only)
1 ½ tbsp Kaffir lime leaf, julienned
few sprigs coriander leaf, for garnish

Method

To poach the crabs, prepare a *court bouillon* (a broth with whatever vegetables and herbs you have to hand, plus a few drops of lemon juice), place the crabs in the broth and poach for 7 to 8 minutes. Remove the crabs; after they cool, extract the meat. Set aside.
Heat the coconut milk until it comes to the boil, add the crab meat until cooked through. When the coconut milk begins to separate, add the remaining ingredients except the garnish.

Serve in bowls, piping hot, and garnish with coriander leaf (and crispy soft shell crab if you have some to hand).

Sundowners Surin-style

Ingredients
60 ml Havana Club rum
1 bar spoon granulated white sugar
50 ml lime juice
18 fresh mint leaves
dash soda water
5 ml Gomme syrup

Mojito

Method

Put the sugar and Gomme in a glass, add the lime juice and rum, and stir, so the sugar dissolves. Place the mint leaves in the middle of your palm and slap them hard before adding them to the glass. Using the bar spoon, rub the leaves onto the walls of the glass (the sugar acts as an abrasive). Add some crushed ice, spread the leaves evenly in the glass, then finish with a dash of soda water and a lime wedge garnish.

Ingredients
45 ml tequila
15 ml Triple Sec
15 ml lime juice
15 ml sugar syrup
1 tbsp passionfruit, frozen

Passionfruit Margarita

Method

Mix all ingredients in a cocktail shaker along with some ice cubes. Pour into a long or martini glass, and garnish with zest of orange.

Ingredients
45 ml Beefeater gin
15 ml Cherry Heering
30 ml lime juice
5 ml grenadine syrup
splash DOM Bénédictine

Surin Sling

Method

Shake all the ingredients in a cocktail shaker along with some ice cubes. Pour into a long glass, top with soda water, and garnish with a lime wheel.

The hexagonal-shaped, black-tiled pool at the Surin is the perfect spot for a poolside cocktail. There's the adjacent Sunset Bar, cooling sand beneath your feet, and the chink of ice on cocktail shaker – plus a gorgeous Surin sunset, of course (see overleaf).

Ingredients

30 ml Absolut vodka
30 ml Cointreau
5 ml lime juice

Kaffir Chilli

Method

Shake all ingredients with ice cubes in a cocktail shaker, then strain into a margarita glass. Garnish with a Kaffir lime leaf and small floating red chilli.

Ingredients

2 thin slices ginger
2 lychees (canned is fine)
60 ml Absolut vodka
20 ml lychee juice
20 ml lemon juice
10 ml Gomme syrup

Ginger Lycheetini

Method

Muddle the ginger in a cocktail shaker, then add the lychees to extract all the juice. To this, add the vodka, juices and Gomme syrup and shake the mix vigorously. Double strain into a martini glass and garnish with a thin slice of ginger.

Ingredients

30 ml Jose Cuervo white tequila
15 ml Triple Sec
35 ml lime juice
10 ml sugar syrup
1 fresh mango, chopped

Mango Margarita

Method

Place all ingredients with some crushed ice into a blender. When fully blended, transfer into a hurricane glass and garnish with a mango slice.

French Flair

Bold, Vibrant Provencal Cuisine

Most of us know a few Provencal dishes — tasty ratatouille, *bouillabaisse* from Marseille, salade niçoise, the garlicky mayonnaise known as aioli, tangy olive tapenade, pistou soup — but what really brings gourmet travellers to Provence is the idea of *terroir*, cooking that is rooted in its locality. This is particularly prevalent here, as the area is large and geographically diverse, yet united by its rocky landscape and *garigue* vegetation.

Garigue is a Provencal word that describes the vegetation known as the *maquis* in Corsica. It's a scrubland of small shrubs that grows on a hard base, needing little water and lots of sun. It is a landscape of rocky terraces, olive trees, wild fennel, along with juniper bushes, bay bushes and *herbes de Provence*. The *garigue* scents and flavours define Provencal cuisine.

In the north around Avignon, you'll find the famous stew or *daube* and a wonderful array of goat's cheeses; in the centre, the cuisine is based around plenty of fresh seasonal vegetables; on the coast, there's a plethora of seafood. Here,

LEFT AND ABOVE Saint-Tropez scenes (clockwise from left): the bell tower of the parish church; typical balcony of an ochre-painted home; clientele sitting outside La Tarte Tropézienne, the famous café on Place des Lices, whose owners invented the eponymous cake; array of fish and crustaceans fresh from the Med set on ice in the daily fish market, beneath the ancient arches of the old port (note the beautiful mosaics); typical cobbled street.

too, anchovies are caught and more often than not cured in salt, preserving and intensifying their flavour. The cuisine is based around slow-cooked meats (often because they are tough), high-quality vegetables, a bit of game, fresh fish and the staples of thyme, oregano, rosemary, chervil and plenty of garlic. It's these ingredients and techniques that give the cuisine its hearty, robust nature.

In the area around Saint-Tropez, there is further regionalisation. As is to be expected in this pretty little port, fish predominates, but there is liberal use of

ABOVE Provencal market fare, clockwise from top left: Spicy dry-cured sausages; mixed olives from the Lubéron area; cinnamon cookies of north African origin; artichokes; garlic cloves; selection of raddishes; asparagus spears; selection of cheeses including a *tomme*, a gourmet sheep cheese from Corsica, and a goat's cheese; a pile of red mullet; sachet of Provence's famous herbs; anchovies, marinated in herbs and olive oil; red bell peppers.

OPPOSITE TOP Invented by a Polish pastry chef (Alexandre Micka) who opened a bakery in Saint-Tropez in 1955, *tarte Tropézienne* is not really a tart at all, but rather a disc of brioche that is sliced and filled with cream. The filling varies, but is almost always flavoured with kirsch.

OPPOSITE BELOW The twice-weekly market sees both locals, known as Tropéziens, and tourists patronising its bustling stalls.

typical Provencal vegetables, such as fennel, tomatoes, courgettes, peppers and aubergines, as well as garlic and anchovies of course. You'll find a little bit of influence from north Africa in some of the dishes, along with the addition of a few spices and saffron. Not to be missed are the round, flat Fougasse breads, often baked with olives or nuts inside. Honey from local beekeepers sweetens desserts, while cheese and rosé wine complete any Saint-Tropez meal.

A visit to the local market in the Place des Lices is a must for any traveller: held twice weekly, it is set amongst rows of 100-year-old plane trees that provide shade on sunny days. It's the place to go to buy olives, breads and tapenades, fresh seasonal vegetables, and organic greens and salad items. In summer, check out peaches and local *gariguette* strawberries; in autumn, there are plenty of wild mushrooms; in spring, tasty, chunky blades of white asparagus.

MUSE HOTEL DE LUXE

To experience the natural beauty of Provence, its beaches, its cuisine, its *je ne sais quoi*, not to mention the glamour and glitz of Saint-Tropez, a trip to MUSE hotel de luxe comes highly recommended. Situated between the pretty hilltop village of Ramatuelle and the port of Saint-Tropez, it is a discreet retreat set within private, walled gardens. With 15 suites, ten with their own private pools, a heated central pool and refined M restaurant, it is quietly stylish.

Just as the incandescent light and colourful landscape attracted such artists as Renoir, Picasso, Matisse and Chagall to the Mediterranean coastline in the past, so does MUSE attract the modern-day creative cognoscenti. Many of these artists discovered their muses in the area around the hotel; today, the hotel's suites are named after such iconic muses as Josephine, Audrey and Lauren, to name a few.

"Terre et mer" is at the heart of the Provencal experience — and cuisine. Fresh, seasonal produce from land and sea forms the basis of hearty fish, meat and veggie dishes, all cooked with high-grade olive oils and plenty of local herbs.

OPPOSITE AND BELOW Scenes from the hotel include the restaurant at dusk (opposite) and some of the various suites (below). An enticing cheese board with two glasses of red wine made in traditional oak casks from a nearby vineyard are laid tantalisingly on a counter. Bon appetit!

LEFT Set in landscaped gardens that use a selection of local plants, cacti and shrubs, MUSE also has some breathtaking views from many of its rooms and suites.

OPPOSITE The hotel's tranquil pool, lined with gazebos and loungers.

Guests cannot help but be inspired at the hotel: against a palette of off-white and beige tones with a touch of milky acquamarine, there is cool French stone flooring, *marmorino* plastered wall-finishes and simple, yet elegant, furniture. Outside the suites, the atmosphere is much the same, with a pleasant poolside bar, loungers dipping their feet into an acqua-toned pool, and gazebos shaded with soft white linens.

Champagne and canapés are served poolside at dusk; crèpes, freshly cooked at the bar, at tea time. For more substantial meals, head to the indoor/outdoor M restaurant, where fresh, seasonal produce forms the basis of a sophisticated menu. As befits the location, Provencal specialties take the lead with freshly-caught seafood cooked with local olive oils and herbs, as well as veggies such as aubergine, peppers and juicy tomatoes. The bread basket is decorated with edible flowers; local rosé wines are served with ice; and all meals are accompanied by friendly, warm service. The chef shares some of his recipes with us overleaf.

Creamy Garigue-scented Risotto of Roast Langoustine

The Garigue is a type of scrubland found in the MUSE vicinity, a mix of forests, woodland and shrubs that flourish in the Mediterranean climate. As such, the term has also found its way into haute cuisine in dishes that have the resinous flavours of the Garigue. This risotto is one such dish — it's redolent of Tropézienne herbs and scents, along with fabulous, fresh-from-the-Med seafood of course.

Serves 6

500 g Arborio rice
1.4 kg langoustines
60 g shallots, finely diced
30 g garlic, finely diced
1 white onion, finely diced
few sprigs fresh thyme
100 g carrots, finely diced
50 g leeks, finely diced
500 ml white wine
1 tbsp tomato paste
100 ml cognac
3 tbsp flour
300 ml crème fraiche
sprig of thyme, for garnish

Method

Clean the langoustines, removing the shell and head. Set aside.

Crush the shells, head, half the thyme, half the garlic, half the shallots, and half the white onion, plus leeks and carrots, all together with a rolling pin, then put in a frying pan over a medium heat and "sweat" for a few minutes, until all the liquid comes out. Add the cognac and flambée. Add the tomato paste, flour and 250 ml of the white wine plus one litre of water. Simmer on a low heat for 1 and a half hours.

Pass the mixture through a seive, retain the liquid. Three quarters will be used for the risotto, one quarter for the sauce at the end.

Place the remaining garlic, shallots, onion and thyme with a little olive oil and rice in a pan, and pan-fry over a hot heat until the rice becomes transparent (2 minutes maximum). Add a little white wine, then a little of the liquid, until it is absorbed into the rice, then continue with the same process until the rice is cooked *al dente*. Do not over-cook.

At the last minute, pan-fry the langoustines for a couple of minutes to cook through. At the same time, mix the crème fraiche with the remaining risotto liquid and white wine, and cook for five minutes until it reduces.

On a plate, put the rice in the centre, the langoustines in the middle and whip up the sauce and pour all around. Garnish with a sprig of thyme in the middle. Serve immediately.

Serves 6
3 fillets red snapper (3 kg)
1.5 kg potatoes
750 g flour
3 eggs
150 g sun-dried tomatoes
120 g black olives, de-seeded and sliced
75 ml Xeres vinegar (a thick Balsamic)
45 g sugar
2 tbsp freshly squeezed orange juice
1 tsp olive oil
1 tsp veal stock powder
salt and pepper, to taste
60 g butter
90 g rocket

Seared Red Snapper with Gnocchi, Black Olives & Sun-dried Tomatoes

Making home-made gnocchi may seem like a chore, but this wonderfully simple recipe should allay any home cook's fears. As long as you follow the instructions to the letter, this recipe will reward you with a hassle-free cooking experience and plenty of fresh, clean Mediterranean flavours.

Method

To make the gnocchi: Peel the potatoes, then boil the potatoes whole for 20 minutes (do not cut because the potatoes should not absorb any water). Remove from pan, purée and mix with the eggs and 675 g of the flour to obtain a pasta-like consistency. Set aside for 30 minutes.

Sprinkle the rest of the flour on a work surface, place the mix on top and roll into sausage-like shapes. Then cut into small gnocchi-style pieces.

Place in a saucepan of boiling water; after two minutes or so the gnocchi pieces will float to the surface. Drain and set aside.

To make the sauce: Put the vinegar and sugar into a saucepan and cook over a medium heat to reduce the mixture until it is caremalised. Add the orange juice, the veal stock powder, salt and pepper and a little knob of butter. Set aside.

To make the fish: Put a little butter and olive oil into a frying pan, then cook the fish one minute on each side, before placing in the oven for a further 4 to 5 minutes until cooked.

Pan fry the gnocchi, sun-dried tomatoes and olives for 2 to 3 minutes until they turn a brownish colour (do not burn); then, just before plating, mix with the rocket and place on one side of the plate. Place the fish on the other side of the plate and serve with the sauce on the side.

Nougat Glacé with Almonds, Hazelnuts and Pinenuts

Frozen nougat or nougat glacé is a dried fruit and nut confection, sweetened with honey, and very similar to an Italian semifreddo. As such, it is the perfect dessert for a hot summer's day. Because it needs six hours to freeze, you can make it the day before you serve it, ensuring an easy pudding for an elegant al fresco lunch party.

Serves 6

750 ml milk
7 egg yolks
zest from 1 ½ oranges
750 ml *crème fraiche*
60 g sugar
7 spoons lavender honey
75 g white raisins
1 pot green tea
75 g hazelnuts, chopped
75 g pinenuts, chopped
75 g almonds, chopped
sprigs redcurrants and mint leaves, for garnish

Method

Soak the raisins in a bowl of green tea, with a splash of rum if you wish.

Pan-fry the walnuts, pinenuts and almonds for 3 or 4 minutes, until they turn a little brown. Set aside.

Mix the egg yolks and sugar thoroughly, then heat up the milk and orange zest. When the milk/orange mix boils, add the egg/sugar mix and the honey, and warm over a medium heat, stirring all the time, until a *crème anglaise* is obtained. Set aside.

Whip the *crème fraiche* until it thickens slightly. Set aside.

Drain the raisins, then mix all the ingredients together, place in a mould and put in the freezer for a minimum of six hours.

Ten minutes before serving, remove the frozen nougat from the mould, slice into six portions, placing each on a plate. Garnish with redcurrants and mint leaves, serve immediately.

Gariguette Strawberries in a crunchy Pastry with Light Vanilla Cream

Gariguette strawberries, slightly smaller than usual strawberries, have a deeper, sweeter, more intense flavour than ordinary fraises. Today, they account for 20 percent of strawberries grown commercially in France, but their natural home is the rocky, sun-baked terrain of Provence.

Serves 6

500 g *gariguettes* strawberries
50 ml whipped cream
I ½ vanilla pods
150 g icing sugar
6 thin slices flaky pastry
20 g butter, melted
6 mint leaves, for garnish

For the coulis

100 g *gariguettes* strawberries
100 g caster suger
4 tbsp water
½ vanilla pod

Method

Clean and slice all the strawberries. Set 100 g aside for the coulis.

Pour the melted butter onto the slices of pastry, and pile the six slices on top of each other. Then cut into six portions and bake in an oven set at a temperature of 180° C for 8 minutes until crispy and golden brown in colour. Remove from oven and set aside to cool.

To make the coulis: Mix 100 g of sliced strawberries with the sugar and water and half a vanilla pod, then warm over a low heat for 10 minutes. Remove the pod, transfer to a blender, and zap until all is liquid and frothy. Put in the fridge for a minimum of one hour.

Whip the cream and 1 ½ vanilla pods together, adding the icing sugar at the end. Do not stop whipping until a soft, creamy whipped consistency is achieved, ie, a Chantilly cream. Remove the pods.

Put a slice of pastry on the plate, then a layer of strawberries, then the Chantilly cream. Repeat, so there are three layers in total. Repeat for the other five portions, then place on separate plates and serve with the coulis on the side and a mint leaf on the top for garnish.

Taste of Summer Rosé de Provence

Provencal wines are justly renowned around the world for their quality and variety, with plenty of spicy, full-flavoured red wines, a scattering of whites, and, most famous of all, the well-known rosés de Provence. Accounting for over 50 percent of Provencal wine production, the rosés, with their light, crisp flavours and beautiful pink complexion, complement both local dishes and climate.

Wine has been made in the region for over 2,500 years, with the first known vineyards being recorded by Caesar in the area around Marseille. The reds and rosés are usually made from Grenache, Syrah and Mourvèdre grape varieties, the whites from Ugni Blanc and Rolle. Justly, the rosés, with their fresh fruit nose and desire to be served chilled, complement much of the cuisine found on the Mediterranean coastline.

As an apéritif, rosé goes well with a zesty tapenade made from finely chopped olives, capers and olive oil or with the speciality of Nice called the *pissaladière*. Resembling a pizza, it is made with bread dough and usually has a topping of lightly browned onions, sardines, anchovies and small black olives. Alternatively, it may be

OPPOSITE Rosé is served with ice at MUSE hotel de luxe; as an accompaniment are some delicious hors d'oeuvres: bread and tapenade, crudités with a Provencal herb dip, tomato concasse and terrine.

ABOVE Late spring sees the vines shooting up beneath the warm sun.

ABOVE RIGHT A glass of rosé goes well with a local goat's cheese, here scented with oregano and thyme and a sprinkling of black pepper.

OVERLEAF The church and harbour at Saint-Tropez.

drunk with any number of Provencal dishes — from seafood to salads and vegetable dishes such as *ratatouille*. On a hot summer's day, there is nothing more delightful than a seafood salad with lashings of olive oil accompanied by a chilled rosé.

Many private wineries and some of the *caves coopératives* open their doors in the summer months for ad hoc tastings: Just round the corner from MUSE is the Château des Marres at Ramatuelle. The owners have been making wine here since 1610 on 66 acres of vineyards — and they are more than happy to welcome visitors. Alternatively, relax at MUSE, munch on some canapés, and savour a glass poolside.

Index of recipes

Starters

Soups

Main Courses (Fish)

Main Courses (Meat)

Desserts

Restaurants, Hotels & Resorts

Gaya Island Resort
Feast Village and Fisherman's Cove
www.gayaislandresort.com

Tanjong Jara Resort
Di Atas Sungei
www.tanjongjararesort.com

Pangkor Laut Resort
Feast Village, Fisherman's Cove, Chapman's Bar, Uncle Lim's Kitchen
www.pangkorlautresort.com

Eastern & Oriental Express
http://www.orient-express.com/web/eoe/eastern_and_oriental_express.jsp

The Green Leaf Niseko Village
Goshiki
www.thegreenleafhotel.com

Hilton Niseko Village
Pirka, The Flame, Melt, Yotei
http://www3.hilton.com/en/hotels/hokkaido/hilton-niseko-village-hotel-CTSNVHI/index.html

Starhill Gallery
Gonbei San, Shook! Kuala Lumpur
http://www.starhillgallery.com/dining

The Swatch Art Peace Hotel
Shook! Shanghai
www.shookrestaurantshanghai.com
www.swatch-art-peace-hotel.com

JW Marriott Kuala Lumpur
Shanghai
http://www.marriott.com/hotels/hotel-information/restaurant/kuldt-jw-marriott-hotel-kuala-lumpur

The Ritz-Carlton, Kuala Lumpur
Li Yen
http://www.ritzcarlton.com/en/Properties/KualaLumpur/Dining/LiYen/Default.htm

Lot 10
Teeq Brasserie, Kong Tai
http://www.lot10.com.my/store_list.asp?floorcat=1
www.teeq.com.my/about_us.asp

The Majestic Malacca
The Mansion, The Bar, The Library
http://www.majesticmalacca.com

Spa Village Tembok Resort, Bali
Wantilan
www.spavillage.com/tembokbali

The Surin, Phuket
Lomtalay, Beach restaurant, Sunset café
www.thesurinphuket.com

MUSE Hotel de Luxe, Saint-Tropez
M restaurant
http://www.muse-hotels.com/ramatuelle/index_en.php

First published in 2013

Published by:
Talisman Publishing Pte Ltd
52 Genting Lane #06-05
Ruby Land Complex 1
Singapore 349560

Art Direction and Design Norreha Sayuti
Designer Foo Chee Ying
Publisher Ian Pringle

Printed in Singapore
ISBN 978-981-07-3352-0